The Chippewa

The Chippewa

Biography of a Wisconsin Waterway

Richard D. Cornell

WISCONSIN HISTORICAL SOCIETY PRESS

Published by the Wisconsin Historical Society Press
Publishers since 1855

© 2017 by the State Historical Society of Wisconsin

The Wisconsin Historical Society helps people connect to the past by collecting, preserving, and sharing stories. Founded in 1846, the Society is one of the nation's finest historical institutions. *Order books by phone toll free:* (888) 999-1669
Order books online: shop.wisconsinhistory.org
Join the Wisconsin Historical Society: wisconsinhistory.org/membership

For permission to reuse material from *The Chippewa* (ISBN 978-0-87020-780-8; e-book ISBN 978-0-87020-781-5), please access www.copyright.com or contact the Copyright Clearance Center, Inc. (CCC), 222 Rosewood Drive, Danvers, MA 01923, 978-750-8400. CCC is a not-for-profit organization that provides licenses and registration for a variety of users.

Cover image by Matt Schrupp

Printed in Canada
Designed by Brian Donahue and Jessica Collette / bedesign, inc.

21 20 19 18 17   1 2 3 4 5

Library of Congress Cataloging-in-Publication Data

Names: Cornell, Richard D., 1945– author.
Title: The Chippewa : biography of a Wisconsin waterway / Richard D. Cornell.
Description: Madison, WI : Wisconsin Historical Society Press, 2017. |
   Includes bibliographical references and index.
Identifiers: LCCN 2016053807 (print) | LCCN 2016055105 (ebook) | ISBN
   9780870207808 (paperback : alkaline paper) | ISBN 9780870207815 (ebook)
Subjects: LCSH: Chippewa River (Wis.)—Description and travel. | Cornell,
   Richard D., 1945—Travel—Wisconsin—Chippewa River. | Chippewa River
   Valley (Wis.)—Description and travel. | Chippewa River (Wis.)—History. |
   Chippewa River Valley (Wis.)—History, Local. | Chippewa River Valley
   (Wis.)—Biography.
Classification: LCC F587.C5 C67 2017 (print) | LCC F587.C5 (ebook) | DDC
   917.75/404—dc23
LC record available at https://lccn.loc.gov/2016053807

For Adam Cahow, PhD,
who encouraged me to take this journey
and advised me along the way,

For the many people along the Chippewa
who trusted me with their stories,

For my children, Andrew, Brian, and Kristen,
and, of course, for my wife, Dixie,
who tolerated much and would rather be in London.

Contents

Introduction   1

Chapter 1 Origins of the Chippewa   5
          From the Ice Age to the Ojibwe

Chapter 2 Writing the River   21
          East Fork, Glidden, and Bear Lake

Chapter 3 Beyond the Water   39
          Return to Glidden

Chapter 4 Where Waters and Cultures Meet   53
          Lake Chippewa Flowage

Chapter 5 Moving Water   84
          Winter

Chapter 6 Reading the River   108
          Bruce

Chapter 7 The Wild Chippewa   118
          The Flambeau River to Jim Falls

Chapter   8 Shaping a River   138
             Jim Falls to Lake Wissota

Chapter   9 Turning Points   151
             Chippewa Falls

Chapter 10 The Sounds of Summer   165
             Eau Claire

Chapter 11 A Storybook Ending   183
             The Lower Chippewa

             Epilogue   202
             Acknowledgments   208
             Notes   211
             About the Author   232

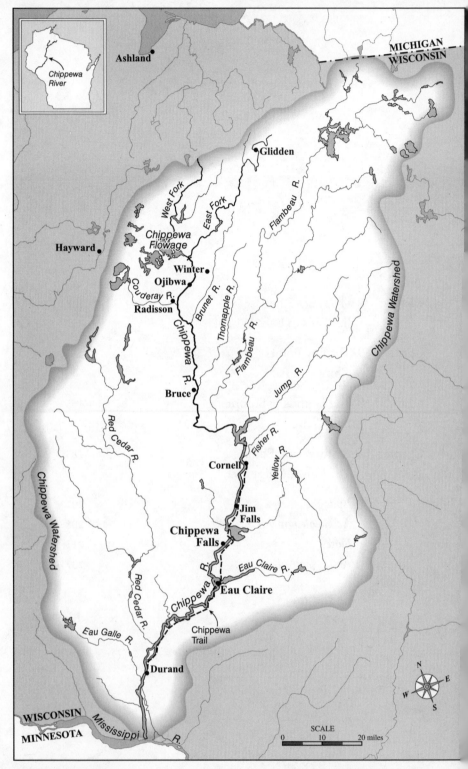

Introduction

Any river is really the summation of the whole valley. To think of it as nothing but water is to ignore the greater part.
—Hal Borland, *This Hill, This Valley*

I have been attracted to moving water most of my life. One of my earliest memories was of the small pools and trickles of water I found in the woods behind my house and below two Lutheran churches in the southern Wisconsin township of Christiana. I was a five-year-old war orphan, which gave me the opportunity to explore the countryside near home alone. When I was eight years old we moved to a forty-acre farm east of Utica, Wisconsin. By that time my mother had remarried, and I had a brother, Dennis, and a sister, Mary Ellen, who were five and seven years younger. Five years is a significant difference when you are young, so I continued my explorations alone.

Near our farm in Utica, a creek emerged between two large oak trees. One day when I was nine or ten, I followed it upstream to its source, where I pushed my face through the watercress and into the bubbling springs. It was the first time I had reached and tasted a source.

In winter the creek became a small trail of ice. Rabbit tracks marked the snow along the frozen creek bed. When spring came I followed the fence lines in search of wild asparagus and studied tadpoles in the creek darting in a small pool above a tiny rock dam.

As an adult, my interest in the sources of rivers continued. Over the course of several decades, I visited the sources of the Mississippi at Lake Itasca; the Loire, flowing from a pipe out of

Mont Gerbier de Jonc in southeastern France; and the Thames at Ashton Keynes in Oxfordshire, England. I saw the Avon at Stratford and stood on the beacon in Painswick in the Cotswolds as the morning sun turned the Severn River silver.

I visited the Derwent River as it flowed below William Wordsworth's boyhood home at Cockermouth. I found myself inspired by Wordsworth's appreciation for the poetry of nature, as when he described his river memories in *The Prelude:*

O Derwent! Traveling over the green plains
Near my "sweet birthplace," didst thou, beauteous stream,
Make ceaseless music through the night and day[1]

Closer to home, I visited the source of the St. Croix. And after my wife, Dixie, and I bought a house in 1984 three blocks from the Chippewa River in Eau Claire, that river became the focus of my exploration and wondering. The University of Wisconsin–Eau Claire walk bridge was our gateway to a bike trail that paralleled the river all the way to the Red Cedar, one of the Chippewa's larger tributaries.

In late October of that year we stood on the bridge and watched as a large community of mallards met in small groups seemingly to plan the future. Watching them I began to hatch my own plan for how the river would be a part of my future. My longtime desire to canoe an entire river from its source returned, and I realized this might be the one.

I drew inspiration from August Derleth's *The Wisconsin*, Peter Ackroyd's *Biography of the Thames*, and Mark Twain's *Life on the Mississippi*. Derleth traced the Wisconsin River and its history, including that of the American Indians and other historical figures connected to it. Ackroyd's deep study of the Thames detailed how the river inspired literature. Twain explored the Mississippi from the perspective of his childhood in Hannibal, Missouri, to his days as a riverboat pilot. I felt the Chippewa deserved a similar study, and I set out to write it.

As I began this project, I decided to keep a journal to record my experiences and thoughts. I wrote my first journal entry in mid-February 1985. The plan was to begin at the source of the Chippewa—where on the road map it became a narrow line and finally disappeared northeast of the town of Glidden. Between 1990 and 2003 my daughter Kristen and I, accompanied occasionally by my sons, Brian and Andrew, and daughter in-law, Kari, paddled the full length of the river, from the source to the point where it empties into the Mississippi. After achieving that goal in 2003, I felt part of the story was missing. I realized that I was unaware of the history and present-day stories that we paddled past. So I returned to Glidden with Andrew and began another downriver journey, this time with the goal of meeting the people who have made their homes along the river and capturing local and historical stories along the way.

I spent time in local museums and libraries up and down the valley and read books that my contacts recommended to me, to learn the stories of the American Indians who first called this land home and the tales of the fur traders, loggers, and other assorted characters who followed. But the most valuable time I spent was in talking to people: in diners, in homes, at local festivals. From these conversations I gathered a history of the Chippewa River Valley that felt as active and fluid as the river. The stories seemed new again every time I dipped in, as each person added a new detail, pointed me in a different direction, or shared an anecdote only they might know.

Early on I saw I had a problem. Where would I stop? Fortunately, I met Adam Cahow, who would become my mentor for this project. While attending a charity event where Dixie had donated some photos, I sat next to a woman who asked me what I did. When I told her I was writing a biography of the Chippewa

River, she told me I had to meet Adam. "He knows everything there is about the Chippewa," she said convincingly. Later, while taking a geological tour sponsored by University of Wisconsin–Eau Claire, I again heard his name. While showing us various formations from the Ice Age, the leader of the tour often remarked something like, "Adam Cahow was the first to understand this."

I first met Adam, who is a retired geology and geography professor from UW–Eau Claire, at his home overlooking the Chippewa. We chatted about my project, and he seemed enthusiastic. When I returned for a second meeting, he presented me with two yellow tablets. On one tablet Adam had written, "The Chippewa River—A Biography by Richard Cornell," followed by a list of suggested chapters he thought I should cover. With his support, my own vision for the book's contents took shape. On the other yellow tablet Adam had written a list of books on rivers that he thought I should read. Among these, *The Streams and Rivers of Minnesota* by Thomas F. Waters, an esteemed river ecologist from the University of Minnesota, deepened my understanding of rivers and my desire to know more. Waters's writings helped me to appreciate that a river is more than a channel of water; it is also everything around it. His ideas cemented my quest in this work to capture stories along the river.

In future meetings, Adam repeatedly cautioned me against casting my net too wide. I was reminded of this while watching a C-SPAN interview with Rick Atkinson, the author of three very comprehensive volumes on World War II. A caller asked him how he decided how much to include. He said that the art of the narrative controlled what he could include and exclude. I tried to follow Atkinson's advice, sticking close to the river as I strung together the stories of the Chippewa River, its valley, and its people. The water is prominent in some stories and recedes into the background in others, sometimes a driving force and at other times a facet of the scenery, but it is the common thread that flows through all of them.

CHAPTER ONE

Origins of the Chippewa

From the Ice Age to the Ojibwe

Names attach themselves to places and stick or fall away. . . .
A name emerges almost automatically from a place as well as
from man and the relationship between name and a thing is
very close.

—JOHN STEINBECK, *THE LOG FROM THE SEA OF CORTEZ*

Arriving in the small town of Glidden, Wisconsin—which has
a population hovering around five hundred residents—I found
the motel with ease. The building sits atop a hill, the word *motel*
spanning its front in large letters, and below it flows the fledgling
East Fork of the Chippewa River.

Pat Bonney, reporter for the *Glidden Enterprise*, picked me up
there early one morning to take me to the source. Pat was born
and raised in Glidden and has a strong interest in the history and
culture of the area. He offered to be my guide in showing me the
little-known true source of the Chippewa.

"Ever been to the wilderness before?" Pat asked me as we prepared to set out. I hesitated, wondering if my river excursions to
this point truly qualified. "So this is your first time," he said, in
answer to my silence.

After driving northwest for about an hour, he guided his pickup into the deep woods in Iron County, until finally we stopped at the edge of three shimmering pools surrounded by tall pines, giving the effect of a cathedral. Small yellow flowers waved on the marshy shore. Pat coaxed the truck up a small hill and left it running.

"We are out of cell phone range, and no one knows we are here," he explained. "We would be in big trouble if I couldn't get it started."

Standing in the silence, I alternated taking photographs and pausing to drink in the moment. I'm an avid reader of poetry, but I found myself thinking that no poem could capture the beauty of that scene. Meanwhile, Pat observed that it was rare for water to pool at this point. It is usually more of a swampy wetland, with water flowing underground from this point toward the Chippewa, but he speculated that the beavers' dams might have trapped some of the water. I felt lucky to see it on a rare occasion when the water had collected aboveground.

"This is the source of the Chippewa," my guide said. "It goes from here to the Mississippi."

While the source of the West Fork is clearly defined by Chippewa Lake, the "true source" of the East Fork is a gathering of small streams: Silver Creek, Augustine Creek, Willerts Creek, Maggie Creek, Mayer Creek, and Schrum's Creek, their names a roll call of early settlers. It is better termed "headwaters" than source. And I'll bet there were trout in some of them.

On our return we stopped at Augustine Creek, and I thought of all these separate strands that flow together to make the one river I had known for so long but had only begun to explore.

⌐∽

The Chippewa begins as a "Y," the West Fork originating in Chippewa Lake, a hundred-acre or so ice-block lake in Bayfield County

The headwaters of the East Fork. RICHARD D. CORNELL

and surrounded by tall pines near Clam Lake. Water trickles from this lake, picks up small tributary streams, and after thirty-eight miles joins its sister near the town of Winter. At this point, the Chippewa is a tranquil stream running in its bedrock channel. While the East Fork is longer, the West Fork is the more expansive of the two where they join in central Sawyer County. The Ojibwe called their village at this meeting point Pahquahwong, meaning "where the river is wide." Today it is the tiny village of Winter, where water gushes from a dam into the river that flows 185 miles to the Mississippi. The story of the dam is a long one, to be explored as we arrive further downriver.

The Chippewa River emerged ten thousand years ago as small streams flowing under and toward the edge of the Chippewa Lobe of the great Laurentide Ice Sheet.[1] In Wisconsin, the glacier branched into five lobes: the Superior, Wisconsin Valley, Langlade,

Green Bay, and Chippewa. The upper branches of the Chippewa River flowed deep in the Chippewa Lobe and emerged as braided streams, small streams that flowed in and out of one another.[2] Over thousands of years, these streams consolidated into one river.

As the earth's climate grew warmer, the glaciers began to melt, creating an enormous rush of meltwater, ice blocks, and boulders. The waters rushed toward the Mississippi, carving the Chippewa Valley along the way.[3] Sedimentary deposits carried by the river poured into the Mississippi, blocking it and forming present-day Lake Pepin. As the ice receded, the permafrost melted, and the resulting tundra became home to the wooly mammoth and musk ox hunted by bands of nomads.[4] Spruce forests emerged, to be replaced, in turn, by white and red pines that would evolve into one of the largest sources of lumber in America, one-sixth that of all pine-bearing tributaries west of the Appalachians.[5]

The Chippewa River could have been named the Anishinaabe or the Ojibwe, if it were truly named for the Native peoples who occupied the land at the time of white settlement. According to Anishinaabe oral tradition, they arrived in the Lake Superior region about fifteen hundred years ago after a five-hundred-year journey from the East.[6] The Anishinaabe received a prophecy that instructed them to follow a white shell until they found a new food source on a body of water. Over several centuries, they followed the prophecy up these rivers and on through Lake Huron to Sault Ste Marie and the rapids of the St. Mary River—the gateway to Lake Superior. In 2010, I visited Trois-Rivières on the St. Lawrence River in Quebec, Canada, and on our way home, we followed the Ottawa River, which the Anishinaabe would have traveled on this epic journey. As we passed over the International Bridge from Canada to Michigan, I looked down at the rapids of St. Mary's—the same rapids that the early Anishinaabe and later explorers paddled through. What a thrill to look down on the rapids and imagine their journey.

Eventually, the Anishinaabe who made their homes in the upper Midwest separated into three groups: the Pottawatomie ("those who keep the fire"), the Odawa ("those who traded," frequently referred to with the anglicized spelling *Ottawa*), and the Ojibwe ("those who keep the faith").[7] The name Ojibwe has several possible origin stories. The most commonly accepted of these is that Ojibwe means "to roast until puckered," referring to the distinctive style of their moccasins.[8] William Warren, a nineteenth-century Ojibwe historian, asserted that this translation actually referred to a method of torture used on captives.[9] The Ojibwe were given other names by the French and English explorers who encountered them after arriving in the New World. The French called them the Saulteur, meaning "people of the rapids," while Chippewa is either an anglicized version of the word *Ojibwe* or an evolution of what the Dakota called the Ojibwe that was adopted by European explorers. Because the Anishinaabe were an oral culture, written documents of the French and English have perpetuated the names and spellings used by white settlers, and the name Chippewa became attached to the river running through Ojibwe lands.

⌁

After several years settled at Sault Ste Marie, the Ojibwe traveled to the safety of an island in Lake Superior, which later came to be known as Madeline Island after an Ojibwe woman who took the name upon marrying a fur trader.[10] Members of the tribe made occasional trips to the mainland. In about 1745, three members of the Bear Clan decided to stay on the mainland, and after a year, several other Ojibwe families joined them. This was on the shore of Lac Coutereille, known as Ottawa Lake or Ottowaw Lake in early descriptions of the area. Soon they established another village at Odawasagaegun on the West Fork of what later became known as the Chippewa River, near where the two forks met.[11] Many believe the name Lac Courte Oreilles, which means "lake of the short ears" in French, came from the numerous bays located on the grand lake, which resemble rounded ears. Others believe this site was named for the manner in which the Odawa residents surgically trimmed their ears.[12]

Ojibwe historian William Warren described the beautiful and resource-rich land of the Ojibwe:

> The O-jib-ways reside almost exclusively in a wooded country; their lands are covered with deep interminable forests, abounding beautiful lakes and murmuring streams, whose banks are edged with trees of the sweet maple, the useful birch, the tall pine, fir, balsam, cedar, spruce, tamarack, poplar, oak, ash, elm, basswood, and all the plants indigenous to the climate in which they reside. Their country is so interspersed with watercourses, that they travel about, up and down streams, from lake to lake, and along the shores of Lake Superior, in their light and ingeniously made birchbark canoes.[13]

By the end of the eighteenth century, the Ojibwe controlled much of present-day Michigan, northern Wisconsin, and Minnesota, as well as large portions of Ontario north of Lake Huron, with Madeline Island and Sault Ste Marie acting as central gathering places. The Ojibwe and Dakota battled for centuries as the two tribes struggled for territory and resources under pressure from white settlement. As of 1776, the Dakota controlled territory along the Chippewa from modern-day Chippewa Falls to the Mississippi, while the upper reaches of the Chippewa Valley remained an important part of the Ojibwe's loosely organized domain. But their land claims were soon to be challenged even further.[14]

~

In July 1534, the French explorer Jacques Cartier, while tacking along the shore of the Gaspé Peninsula, was suddenly surrounded by forty or more canoes of Micmac, an American Indian band native to eastern Canada.[15] They waved pelts on sticks, clearly eager to trade. The following day they traded fur pelts for knives, cutlery, and a red hat for their chief. Some of the women sold the furs on their backs and went naked. Cartier returned to France and sold the furs for a fortune. The fur rush was on.

From the mid-1600s to around 1812, the Chippewa River was an integral part of the network of rivers facilitating trade between the Great Lakes and the Mississippi.[16] From La Pointe—the main trading area—travelers would paddle into Chequamegon Bay, up Fish Creek to the White River, and on to Lake Owen and the headwaters of the Namekagon River. And from there traders could portage to the Chippewa and on to the Mississippi—a route that would take them past Lac Courte Oreilles.[17]

The first person to write his experience with the Chippewa River was the French explorer Pierre-Esprit Radisson.[18] In the fall of 1659, he and his brother-in-law Medart Chouart, Sieur des Groseilliers, arrived on Chequamegon Bay, having traveled the common route from Trois-Rivières up the St. Lawrence to the Ottawa River, and across Lake Huron to Sault Ste Marie.

They built a cabin, possibly the first on the lake, near present-day Ashland. A facsimile of this cabin is located at Maslowski Beach on the outskirts just west of town. Radisson, a young man with a high level of emotional intelligence and cultural awareness, was one of a number of young men recruited by Samuel de Champlain with the intention to engage with and learn the native culture. In his journal Radisson would arrogantly declare, "We were Caesars, being nobody to contradict us."[19] This provided historian Grace Nute the title to her classic book on Radisson

A replica of the Radisson-Groseilliers cabin stands in Maslowski Park in Ashland.
RICHARD D. CORNELL

and des Groseilliers, *Caesars of the Wilderness*.[20] In 1660 they explored inland as far as Odawasagaegun.[21] During this time they were very close to the West Fork of the Chippewa River, making them the first known European explorers to observe the infant river that had long been important to the Ojibwe.

Radisson was not focused on rivers; he was following the money—that is, beaver pelts. His goal was to build relationships with American Indians who knew where the beavers lived, and he depended on them for his survival. He and des Groseilliers spent the winter of 1660 lodging with the Odawa along the Couderay, a Chippewa tributary, unaware they were at the head of a big river leading to the Mississippi—and eventually to the Gulf of Mexico. It would be others who would begin to describe the form and shape of the Chippewa, from the river's mouth to the Mississippi.

Father Louis Hennepin was the first white explorer to paddle the Chippewa upstream from its mouth.[22] After being released as a prisoner by the Dakota in 1680, he descended the Mississippi from Lake Mille Lacs, on the way giving St. Anthony Falls in Minneapolis its name. He arrived at the mouth of the Chippewa, which he referred to by its earlier name, Buffalo River, when describing it in *Narrative of the Voyage to the Upper Mississippi*:

Half a league below the lake of Tears [Lake Pepin], on the south side, is Buffalo river, full of turtles. It is so called by the Indians on account of the number of buffalo (*boeufs*) found there. We followed it for ten or twelve leagues; it empties impetuously into the river Colbert [Mississippi], but as you ascend it, it is constantly gentle and free from Rapids.[23]

In 1767, Jonathan Carver, who fought with the British in the French and Indian War, arrived at the mouth of the Chippewa. A self-taught cartographer, he was commissioned by Robert Rogers, who led the well-known and successful militia unit known as Rogers' Rangers.[24] After traveling down the Wisconsin River to Prairie du Chien, Carver proceeded up the Mississippi to the Minnesota River, where he spent the winter with the Dakota. On his return trip in early spring, he witnessed a meeting of American Indian leaders in a cave now known as Carver's Cave. On May 28, 1767, Carver wrote in his journal, "Came to where the Chippewa River joined the Mississippi," then described his journey upstream past large plains populated with thousands of buffalo, for which the river had been named.[25] According to John Vanek, it was likely Carver who first started calling the river the Chippewa.[26] He was the first white man to canoe the river from its mouth to the Couderay River and the first to write of his trek upriver.

Carver traveled to London in 1769 hoping to sell his manuscript of this adventure on the Chippewa. The four versions of his journals are preserved in the British Library, and the latter three were developed into book form, first published in 1778. According to the journals, he began his journey on the Chippewa at Lake Pepin and steered toward Ottawa Lake, with the assistance of an Indian pilot.[27] On June 4, 1767, Carver wrote of the next part of his journey:

> Came to the great medows or plains. Here I found excellent good land and very pleasant country. One might travel all day and only see now and then a small pleasant grove of oak and walnut. This country is covered with grass which affords excellent pasturage for the buffeloe which here are very plenty. Could see them at a distance under the shady oaks like cattle in a pasture and sometimes a drove of a hundred or more shading themselves in these groves at noon day.[28]

Carver must have endured the rapids because he reports that he paddled and portaged his way upstream. Describing the wilderness leading here, he wrote, "After we left the plains till we came to this town for upwards of a hundred miles is a most dreary wilderness of trees." On June 22, Carver turned left, away from the Chippewa and up the present Couderay River. He arrived at what he called a castle, by which he meant a cluster of buildings standing on both sides of the river.[29] In 1745, the Ojibwe had established a village on the shore of the West Fork at an abandoned Odawa village.

A more descriptive account of exploring the early Chippewa River was provided by C. H. Cooke a century later. In 1868, Civil War veterans C. H. Cooke, George Sutherland, and S. A. Hall, head of the Old Wesleyan Seminary in Eau Claire, purchased a canoe from an Ojibwe at Jims Falls (today known as Jim Falls), and headed upstream. Cooke described the scene in his diary, invoking the poetry of Lord Byron:

All afternoon the walls of deep green pines crowding close to
the river gives one a feeling of being a discoverer or a pioneer.
For ages, no doubt, this silent river, fringed by these eternal
pines, had run on unresting, unhasting, and unspent. There is
something glorious in the loneliness of this glorious solitude.
On my asking George to recall something from the poets ap-
propriate to the scene, he at once started on the lines famous
in "Childe Harold"...

   Following this the professor dropped his stick from pok-
ing up the fire and clapped his hand. Curiously enough, a lot
of crows overhead, winging their silent way across the river,
observing us and startled by our clapping, set up a chorus of
cawing, protest or approval we were uncertain which.[30]

Prior to the arrival of European fur traders and priests, the Ojibwe
sustained themselves with hunting and fishing, growing seasonal
crops such as beans, corn, squash, and potatoes, and harvesting
wild rice and maple syrup. They traveled in birchbark canoes,
lived in smoky homes made of deer skin and birchbark, and
trapped animals for their furs. When Frenchmen arrived, the
Ojibwe became active traders, exchanging fur pelts for a variety
of European weapons, metal tools, and other goods. The hunt for
pelts pushed the tribe further inland, encroaching on the territory
of the Dakota, with whom the Ojibwe had clashed off and on for
centuries. Guns gained from the fur trade now gave the Ojibwe
a competitive advantage over their rival.

   Historian Mary Lethert Wingerd describes the Ojibwe as
clever negotiators and traders who were willing to cooperate with
and strongly challenge the government when their rights and
treaty obligations were violated. She quotes Daniel Stanchfield, a
timber cruiser who in 1850 observed that the Ojibwe were "more

true and honorable than most white men with who I came in contact with on the frontier."[31]

But whatever their negotiation skills, the American Indians suffered great consequences. In 1825, the US government brokered a peace treaty between the warring tribes, but the pact was a step toward US seizure of Native lands. Beginning with the Jackson administration and the Indian Removal Act of 1830, the push was to relocate all tribes west of the Mississippi. In the treaties of 1837 and 1842, the Ojibwe ceded logging and copper-mining rights in the area south of Lake Superior that encompass the headwaters of the Chippewa, in exchange for a small annuity. The Ojibwe saw the deal as a lease arrangement, not a permanent sale of their land. They planned to continue to live, hunt, and fish on the land. But William Medill, commissioner of Indian Affairs in 1845, "suggested evicting the Chippewas from northern Wisconsin as a means of promoting their 'civilization.'"[32]

On February 6, 1850, President Zachary Taylor issued an executive order that invalidated the treaties and ordered the Ojibwe to move to the west side of the Mississippi:

> The privileges granted temporarily to the Chippewa Indians
> of the Mississippi by the Fifth Article of the Treaty made
> with them on the 29th of July 1837 "of hunting, fishing and
> gathering the wild rice, upon the lands, the rivers, and the
> lakes included in the territory ceded" by that treaty to the
> United States . . . are hereby revoked; and all of the said Indi-
> ans remaining on the lands ceded as aforesaid, are required to
> remove to their unceded lands.[33]

The order was strongly resisted by both Ojibwe and some white allies. An editorial in the Sault Ste Marie newspaper argued against the president's action: "This unlooked for order has brought disappointment and consternation to the Indians throughout the Lake Superior country and will bring them most disastrous consequences."[34]

Several members of the Wisconsin legislature, religious leaders, regional newspapers, and others also lobbied for the Ojibwe to be able to stay on their land. Meanwhile, Chief Buffalo, a leader of the Ojibwe, dispatched scouts to find out if his tribal members had been engaged in any conflicts with whites that would have provoked their removal. Finding none, the Ojibwe planned to stay in their home.[35]

Their efforts proved unsuccessful, as Bureau of Indian Affairs subagent John S. Watrous in Wisconsin and territorial governor Alexander Ramsey of Minnesota hatched a plot to move the Ojibwe to Minnesota.[36] In 1850, Watrous, Ramsey, and others conspired to change the location for delivery of their annuity payment—paid to the tribes by the federal government as part of a treaty—to Sandy Lake in Minnesota. Their plan was to lure the Lake Superior Chippewa tribes into Minnesota and trap them there for the winter. They scheduled the payment for late October and ordered that the Ojibwe should appear at Sandy Lake with their families to receive their due.[37]

The Ojibwe chose to send only their men. When they arrived, the annuity was not there, and neither were sufficient supplies. It is estimated by Ojibwe leaders that around 170 died at Sandy Lake from disease and starvation. Another 230 died on the journey home.[38]

In the spring of 1852 Chief Buffalo, his interpreter Benjamin Armstrong, a young leader named Oshoga, and four others traveled to Washington, DC, to meet with newly elected President Millard Fillmore.[39] In his book, Armstrong wrote that the young braves were angry. Chief Buffalo asked the president, "Is it not the obligations of the white men to fulfill their contracts?" Oshoga made the following speech:

Chief Buffalo, principal chief of the Lake Superior Ojibwe Band, who lived from 1759 to 1855. WHI IMAGE ID 3957

It is generally the case with the white men, when they have selected a spot to dwell at, that they begin to consider and look around them, to see what obstacles are in their way. They begin to cut away the underbrush and bad trees, in order to make the land level and smoothe so that nothing will come in contact to hurt their feet, they see good trees and they are allowed to stand & live, & they are not cut down. We beseech

An illustration from Benjamin Armstrong's book Early Life Among the Indians *shows Chief Buffalo and the rest of the Ojibwe delegation that went to Washington, DC, in 1853.* WHI IMAGE ID 3351

you to do towards us as you do, allowing the good trees [the Wisconsin Chippewa] to stand and live in your domain. And furthermore we pray, that in accordance to that, we so fully understood that our annuities be paid to us at La Point & that they may be continued there.[40]

Following this meeting, President Fillmore created the Wisconsin Chippewa reservations: Bad River, Red Cliff, Lac du Flambeau, Mole Lake, St. Croix, and Lac Courte Oreilles. It is possible that Chief Buffalo's intervention prevented a war, although the Ojibwe still lost much in the way of rights to Wisconsin's land and resources.

Today the Lac Courte Oreilles Reservation is near the shore of the Lake Chippewa Flowage formed by the Winter Dam on the

Chippewa River, another broken treaty promise. Chief Buffalo, a baptized Christian, died in 1855 and was buried in La Pointe on Madeline Island, the spiritual home of the Ojibwe.[41] Much of the Lake Superior region, including portions of modern-day Minnesota and Wisconsin, was named La Pointe County. In 1860 a portion of this land became Ashland County, where the town of Glidden and the headwaters of the Chippewa reside.

◦~◦

CHAPTER TWO

Writing the River

East Fork, Glidden, and Bear Lake

The search for the origins of rivers has long fascinated mankind.

—Thomas Waters, *Wildstream*

The source of the East Fork of the Chippewa River flows from a shimmering pond surrounded by tall, verdant pine trees. Water trickles from there and joins a number of small streams to form the fledgling river. But this was not the place I first believed to be the source.

When I started to contemplate my canoe adventure I imagined a solo journey. As I thought more about it, I realized it would be safer and more fun to have a partner. At some point I realized that if my daughter, Kristen—who I called KC—would join me, it would be an opportunity to spend some much-needed time with her since I separated from her mother. I wanted to create a memory. As it turned out, it became a source of memories for most of my kids. Our journey began on Father's Day 1990. I picked up KC at 5 a.m. at her mother's house in Eau Claire. Half asleep, she made her way to the car with her fishing rod and sleeping bag. While she slept in the passenger seat, I watched the sunrise as we headed north on Highway 53.

KC with our canoe as we began this journey on Father's Day in 1990.
RICHARD D. CORNELL

Four hours later, we arrived at Musky Pete's restaurant on the outskirts of the small town of Glidden. I had previously scouted the area and learned that the Mackenberg Bridge north of town was close to the source. The people in the restaurant agreed, and two of them followed us to the bridge to take our car back to Glidden so it would be waiting there for us. We unloaded our red, eighteen-foot Mad River Canoe and watched our car head back to Glidden. The river at this point was ten to fifteen yards wide, about the size of a large stream. We slid our craft down the bank and climbed in.

After about an hour of paddling upstream from the bridge, we were blocked. The water to the left was obstructed by fallen branches; the water to the right was clear and quiet. The most active water was coming out of the center channel. We checked out the right channel, which started as an oval about sixty yards across before narrowing into a path through the weeds. We got just a few yards up the center branch when a large fallen tree blocked our path. The water was three to four feet deep in this narrow passage, lined by swampy land on each side.

"Does this feel like a place where a river is born?" I asked.

"To me it feels like a great place for a tire swing," KC answered.

We sat here for a while enjoying the break from paddling, and the red canoe rocked gently in the dark water. I wanted to remember this feeling forever.

Our eighteen-foot, red fiberglass canoe was patterned after the design of the usually fourteen-foot Ojibwe canoes that preceded us downriver more than a hundred years before. The Ojibwe birchbark canoes were fashioned from nature. The bark taken from a large tree was big enough to fashion one canoe. In his poem *Hiawatha's Sailing*, Henry Wadsworth Longfellow captured the spirit of this elegant craft:

All the lightness of the birch-tree,
All the toughness of the cedar,
All the larch's supple sinews;
and it floated on the river,
Like a yellow leaf in Autumn
Like a yellow water-lily[1]

My red canoe doesn't derive itself from the surrounding environment in the same way as its Ojibwe predecessor, but I like to think it floats like a leaf or a lily just the same. My thoughts drifted in that direction as we rested and considered our quest for the day.

The late University of Minnesota professor Dr. Thomas F. Waters, who wrote prolifically about rivers and streams, had his own thoughts about what constitutes a river's source. He told the story of Henry Schoolcraft's 1832 quest to find the source of the

Mississippi in *The Streams and Rivers of Minnesota*. An Ojibwe guide led Schoolcraft to Lake Itasca, but he wondered if the lake was truly the source. Small streams may flow into the lake, but where does the water in the streams originate? The drop of water on a pine needle might be a waterway's true source, as Waters later wrote.[2]

Confident at this point that KC and I had discovered the Chippewa's source—or at least as close to it as we would be able to get by canoe that day—I turned us around.

This was the first moment of a journey that would take thirteen years. At the time, KC was eighteen, and I was forty-six. We both led busy lives, hers as a student first at Memorial High School in Eau Claire and then at University of Wisconsin–Stevens Point, where she majored in elementary education and English language learning. After graduation she joined the staff of Farmington and started the first English language learning program for the district. From there she earned a master's in urban education from Hamline University in St. Paul. I worked as an organization development consultant and traveling teacher during the course of our trip. We managed at least a day a year, sometimes more, on the river.

On our way downstream, we passed under the bridge and encountered our first tangle of downed trees and brush. It was obvious that our journey would be a push, pull, and drag experience. Some trees at the river's edge had fallen across the river, victims of the depth fluctuations that cause the soil around the roots to erode. When a tree falls, the branches catch and hold other twigs and branches that are floating downriver, creating massive floating brush piles.

We encountered a number of such tangles—a taxonomy of sorts of the local vegetation. There were the fresh-fallen trees with their leaves still intact. Then there were the solitary trees that had died long before they fell into the river. You could still make out their branch system, though time and water current had stripped the bark away, leaving a smooth wood surface. In some places, the brush piles looked more deliberate, and it was obvious that beavers had been at work. After several hours of climbing in and out, wading, pushing, dragging, and occasionally paddling, the steeple of the Most Precious Blood Catholic Church and the silver balloon of the Glidden water tower emerged above the trees. We pulled out at the gentle bank below the Grant Street Bridge. A mallard couple, similar to one we had seen slightly upriver, took flight, made a long lazy circle, and headed upriver. Had they accompanied us during our expedition?

Glidden, a town of around five hundred people, is the first small town on the Chippewa. With the exception of Chippewa Falls and Eau Claire, the Chippewa is defined by small towns. Not content to be merely small, many offer some claim to greatness.

Gliddenites claim the title Black Bear Capital of Wisconsin. At 665 pounds, the largest one ever shot in the state growls out at us from inside a glass case next to the Bruin Restaurant. The bear was killed by a hunter on November 23, 1963. They also lay claim to the largest pine tree log, which rests on an old logging sled on a hill above the town. The sign on the log claims that the twenty-foot-long cut from a 450-year-old white pine weighed in at three and a half tons. Beyond these more famed landmarks, the Glidden History Museum has a large collection of vintage chain saws. After all, this is logging country. Like many towns along the Chippewa, Glidden can trace its very beginnings to the timber industry.

As beavers grew scarce and felted beaver fur slowly gave way to silk as the preferred material for making top hats, the fur trade ground to a halt by about the time Wisconsin became a state in

1848.[3] But the French Canadians who had come to trade for pelts found a new calling, the white pine. The banks of the Chippewa and its tributaries were lined with millions of acres of these trees, full of promise like living gold. One-sixth of all Wisconsin's pine grew east of the Mississippi along the Chippewa and its creeks and tributaries. The process was simple: cut down the trees, saw them into sixteen-foot lengths, float them downriver to a sawmill, make the lumber into a raft, and float it to the Mississippi and on to St. Louis.

In 1828, twenty years before Chief Buffalo's courageous and historic journey, the first rudimentary sawmill was built on the Red Cedar River near present-day Menomonie.[4] Following the treaty of 1837, which opened up much of Wisconsin for logging, a group of businessmen in Prairie du Chien dispatched French immigrant Jean Brunet to build a mill on the Chippewa. He constructed his mill at what is today Chippewa Falls and built a cabin twenty miles upstream, below present-day Cornell. According to William Bartlett, Brunet is the first pioneer and could be called the founder of the Chippewa Valley.[5] I would learn more about Brunet's fascinating story when I reached his hometown at Cornell.

The first men to carry their axes into the woods were French Canadians who had immigrated south following the end of the fur-trading era. The industry also attracted skilled loggers and experienced entrepreneurs from Maine and Vermont, while immigrants from Germany, Norway, and Poland also saw the axe as a path to building a stake to start their own farm. A worker in the woods from Madison likened sleeping in a lumber camp to snoring in seven languages. The Ojibwe were also fully engaged as lumberjacks, felling the trees, pushing them to the river, and guiding the logs downstream. By 1880, the federal census reported the following profile of workers in the woods: 1,805 American Indians, 473 British Americans, 275 Germans,

89 Irish, and 106 from other countries.[6] Common laborers received from fifteen to twenty dollars per month and board. Log drivers on the river received two to three dollars per day plus meals.[7]

Trees were felled, first by axe and then by two-man saws. They were cut into sixteen-foot lengths and brought by horse-pulled sleds along ice paths to a river or dammed-up creek, where they were stacked.[8] When the ice went out, the piles of logs collapsed and tumbled their way down the river through the rapids to the mills in Chippewa Falls and Eau Claire. Output was measured in board feet—one foot long, one foot wide, and an inch or so thick. The annual production of the Chippewa Valley doubled from 1858 to 1884.[9]

Some of the ambitious lumber capitalists who braved the unruly water and unpredictable economy of the Chippewa grew wealthy and eminent in the process of forging the lumber industry along its banks.[10] Their names remain on towns, such as Thorp and Stanley; a university, Stout; and several parks, Carson, Irvine, and Randall. History remembers the rest: Allen, Kaiser, Pound, Ingram, Weyerhaeuser, and Knapp. Most of the entrepreneurs eventually moved on to other forests, and on Interstate 5 in Portland, drivers still see the name Weyerhaeuser written large on buildings along the Columbia River. But those who stayed grew the timber industry, attracting immigrant workers to the woods, who went on to start farms and families and built the river towns that continue to roll along.

In the 1950s, historian Walker Wyman discovered Louie Blanchard, a retired lumberjack living on a cutover farm on the Chippewa at Cornell. Blanchard was born in 1872, worked as a logger from 1888 to 1912, and died in 1959. Blanchard's story, though highly edited, is a firsthand, rich treasure of a logger's life. Here he describes the watery logging network of the Chippewa Valley:

Pretty near everything was made of wood in those days, and
a lot of it came out of the Chippewa pineries. It seemed that
every river and crick and lake was made for this purpose.
They seemed to be laid out so that every log could find its
way to market. Every territory that had trees on it had a crick
running through it, and the cricks ran into bigger ones until
finally they reached the Mississippi River. I'm not much on
religion, but it sure looks like the rivers and lakes of Wisconsin was laid out for a mighty high purpose. The loggers would
take the timber off of one territory at a time and go right up
the rivers and cricks doing it. They moved up the Chippewa
to the Eau Claire and up its cricks, then to the Yellow and its
cricks, on to the Jump and the north and south branches of
the Flambeau and all their cricks, until the last pine had been
cut and floated down the river.[11]

Over time, the popularity of pine caused its scarcity close to
the river. As the distance between the forests and the river increased, it became cost-effective to build railroads through the
forest rather than carry the loads by water. By the 1880s, most of
the Chippewa's logs were being transported to the mills by rail.[12]

The last lumber raft drifted down the Chippewa from Eau
Claire in 1905. Seventy years of cut-and-run lumbering created
thousands of acres of cutover land. George Perkins Marsh, author of *Man and Nature* (1864) and considered by many to be
the country's first environmentalist, observed, "When the vast
forests disappeared . . . rivers famous in history have shrunk to
humble brooklets."[13] It became clear that the land needed to be
restored. The US Forest Service was formed and established the
Chequamegon and Nicolet National Forests in the early 1930s.
The Chippewa flows through much of it today.

The entrepreneurial hunger for profits drove its way into the
pine forest with no regard for its consequences. August Derleth

quotes a passage from Merk's *Economic History of Wisconsin* describing the destruction of Wisconsin's forests beginning in the Civil War decade:

> The enormous waste that was going on in logging, sawing, and marketing lumber was likewise regarded as of little moment. Every step in the transformation of the pine tree into the sawed board was marked by improvidence. The log choppers cut the trees high, wasting long stumps, while the sawyers in dividing the fallen pine into logs wasted many feet of clear timber at the top. Young growth was given scant consideration, while windfalls that were not in prime condition were left to rot. It has been estimated that as a result of careless logging and fires not more than forty per cent of the magnificent forest that once clothed northern Wisconsin ever reached the sawmill.[14]

When the first timber cruisers arrived in the Chippewa Valley in 1830, the pine forests appeared to be an endless resource. By 1905, when the last lumber was floated down the Chippewa, Wisconsin was importing wood from the south and west.[15]

When people compete for profits, when workers compete to earn money to feed their families, the story is always the same, be it the Wisconsin forests or the English Channel where fishermen competed with one another to catch the last fish; unless stopped by government regulation, the rush to gobble it all up continues. An 1876 letter to the *Northwestern Lumberman* described this situation in the Wisconsin north: "You have scolded the lumbermen for cutting so much timber. Well, we have cut a great deal, but what can we do about it: Quit? Who will pay the debts or feed those who are now working for us? When we are out of timber, then we will curtail. But until that day, never. So help us Moses!"[16]

For the price of its earlier white pine forests, the Chippewa

Valley drew a collection of immigrant workers and entrepreneurs
to Wisconsin, joining the area's American Indians, European explorers, traders, and priests. It started with the ring of the axe on
a cold February day or the whine of a saw making lumber, which
attracted countless newcomers who dreamed of someday starting a farm, opening a shop, or making a living in the valley some
other way. Businesses sprang up to serve the newcomers—shoes,
beer, bars, and saw blades—and communities were born. As one
lumberman looked back and reflected:

> I'll stand by the gate and keep watching for those
> Who come with the smell of pine on their clo's
> For even in heaven I'll wait, I will,
> The smell of the sawdust that comes from the mill[17]

The small towns born of the lumber era remained. Among
them was the first sizable town to appear along the river—Glidden. As Wisconsin's pine forests thinned out in the latter part
of the nineteenth century, loggers turned to hardwoods. These
heavier logs could not float down the river like pine, so the logging
industry relied even more on the newly built railroads for transportation. In early 1870, communities from Portage to Ashland
passed bonding bills to fund the Wisconsin Central Railroad, to
be routed between the Chippewa and Wisconsin River systems.[18]
After a few false starts, the Wisconsin Central Railroad plotted
Glidden in its present form and changed its name from Chippewa
Crossing to Glidden in honor of a now-long-forgotten railroad official. The rails arrived in Glidden in 1877, thus launching the town.

To attract immigrants to northern Wisconsin, the railroad
published a brochure in English and German that was widely
distributed in Europe. The brochure promised "a remarkable
summer climate like that of Venice free of consumptive threats.
Here the agricultural capital of America would rise."[19] While the

promotional literature might have overstated its promise, at its peak in the late 1800s Glidden boasted a gas station, bank, drug store, grocery story, clothing store, roller rink, restaurant, and a few bars. Glidden suffered a decline along with the lumber industry, though it experienced a brief renaissance during the fishing boom in the late 1920s, when fishermen from Chicago and other cities arrived to town via the Wisconsin Central and were bused fifty miles to the resorts of the Chippewa Flowage.

During my many visits to Glidden, I lobbied them to do more to claim the Chippewa as one of their points of local pride. I envisioned a sign there declaring, "Glidden, Source of the Chippewa River." But over time, I realized the difficulty of claiming that conclusively. When questions about the source of the Chippewa first took hold of me in the 1970s, I was standing on a walk bridge at the University of Wisconsin–Eau Claire, wondering where the river flowing beneath my feet originated. I imagined a pristine pool surrounded by stately white pines, hundreds of miles upstream. I was unaware at the time that the Chippewa had more than one source.

Early in our explorations, KC and I located the source of the West Fork near Clam Lake. The owner of a bar in town gave us directions. After an anxiety-filled ride across hilly country, much of it through deep sand, we reached Lake Chippewa, an undeveloped, hundred-acre, ice-block lake northwest of Clam Lake. We stood on its shore listening to the silence, knowing that somewhere south of where we stood the West Fork flowed out of it, but unable to get anywhere near it with the maps we possessed.

On July 10, 1993, after a three-year break, we resumed our project. KC had a friend who was the niece of Robert and Matt Hart, owners of the *Glidden Enterprise*. I called Matt, and he agreed to shuttle our cars for our next leg.

We met the brothers for breakfast at the Glidden Hotel. According to Matt, few people came up to canoe the river. Back in the 1960s, lots of "hippies" reportedly lived in the woods. He told us about one couple who came to write children's books but couldn't make a go of it, so they started a business, Winter Woods, making starter sticks for fireplaces and distributing Christmas wreaths made by the women of the town. They also sold bags of stones they collected on the shores of Lake Superior.

Matt recalled that during the 1960s, someone had placed canoes in the lakes nearby so folks could use them to travel from lake to lake through the forest. He talked about the day the government came to town to build the ELF (extremely low frequency) system, a network of underground antennas that snaked its way from Clam Lake through the forest and along the river. It was used to communicate with submarines all around the world; satellites later replaced the system. Some of the local hippies, and even some old-timers, protested the military intrusion, but "we needed every job we could get," Matt recalled.

The Harts discouraged us from picking our journey back up at Glidden; the river was choked with too many fallen trees. They suggested we begin at the Shanagolden Bridge a few miles from Glidden, and given our previous experience, we agreed.

Below Glidden the river curves in a large V, going south for some distance then turning north, winding around drumlins. I rode with Robert, while KC rode with Matt. As we made our way downstream Robert expressed his fears that when he and Matt were gone, no one in the family would want to keep the *Enterprise* going. Even as many people have turned to the internet for most of their news, small-town print newspapers such as this remain an important source of information about community happenings, and he wondered who would carry on that tradition. Matt Hart passed away in 2002, but he would be pleased to know that Pat Bonney and members of the Hart family are keeping the paper going.

At the Bay Road Bridge, the ELF wires crossed the river and someone was fly-fishing. As we were unloading our canoe, Matt pointed to a very large pine tree on the opposite bank. A woman who was secretary of the Shanagolden Logging Company had planted it. She returned from her home in New York when she was ninety-six to do so. Matt said tears rolled down her cheeks as she gazed at the tree and remembered her days working at the short-lived mill, the brief but tragic history of which I would find out more on later.

We said good-bye to the Hart brothers and pushed off. "You will have clear sailing from here down," Robert assured us.

Indeed, the river was much clearer than we had seen north of Glidden. After floating under the bridge, we encountered a small set of rapids and got stuck in the rocks. We scrambled out, repositioned ourselves, and paddled on. A lowland forest of mixed conifers and deciduous trees appeared on our right. Dense forest lined the bank. The ground was high along one side of a drumlin and low on the other. Conifers occupied the high land on one shore, while deciduous trees covered the low land on the other. Following a second set of rapids, we saw that the high ground had shifted to the right. The river widened, and old cabins appeared on the shore. We arrived at Pelican Lake, one of five lakes we would encounter before reaching the dam near the village of Winter. A patch of tall grass concealed some honking birds. Two men in a bass boat were casting large, heavy lures. After three and a half hours of paddling, we arrived at Stockfarm Bridge. The Harts had dropped off our vehicle there, with the keys hidden under a cup on the front seat.

For our next leg, a friend, Dennis Aney, offered to take us to Stockfarm Bridge and pick us up downstream in two days. We launched from the bridge at 3:30 p.m. It was August 21, plenty of summer sun remaining. The day also held shadow for me. My father had been killed in Bellegarde, France, on this date and time of day in 1944.

❧

It was easy paddling at first, with a few intermittent small rapids. The water was low, and we often scraped on the rocks. Our plan was to paddle until 7:30 p.m. before looking for a place for the night. The shore was often lined with rocks and boulders, showing more remnants of the glacial age than upstream. Four- and five-foot boulders were common. Adam Cahow had informed me the upper Chippewa flows over bedrock. We were seeing an example.

We paddled into Bear Lake about 6:45. It's a round, 220-acre musky and walleye lake, about a mile and a half across. Houses lined the shore to our left as we entered the lake. The ground to our right was solid forest dotted with No Trespassing signs. We circled the lake looking for a place to camp, and I started to consider the unseen people who made their homes here and how little I knew of them at this point. What were their stories, and how were they connected to the water flowing nearby? A few people were fishing from their docks, but we decided not to inquire about camping possibilities. The day was heading toward 8 p.m. and the sun was sliding rapidly toward the horizon. With no options in sight on either shore, we started looking for the exit channel.

As we studied the shoreline, I mused that it would not have looked much different in 1937, when all the land on the north side was owned by champion middleweight wrestler Charlie Fischer. Like many early residents of this area, Charlie cut his teeth on logging, but an oversized ambition led this underdog to bigger things. And still late in life, he found himself called back to the waters of northern Wisconsin.

Fischer was born in 1898 on a farm near Butternut. By the time he was twelve, he was already a lumberjack. In the summer of 1910 an itinerant wrestler came to a band concert at G.A.R. Park in Butternut to take on all comers for cash. Twelve-year-old Fischer, standing five feet two inches tall, stepped out of the crowd. He made a dive for his opponent's underpinnings with cool, calculating courage, upsetting the larger man, and much to the bully's surprise, had him flat on his back in a matter of seconds.[20]

Though Charlie enjoyed working in the forest, he also longed to see the world beyond northern Wisconsin, and at nineteen he headed west to work as a logger in the state of Washington. After a brief return to Butternut, his hunger for adventure drew him to Chicago, where he got a job at Henry Pfund's beverage distributing company. Pfund had an interest in professional wrestling and when he saw Charlie effortlessly carrying heavy barrels,

Champion middleweight wrestler Charlie Fischer. WALTER B. FISCHER

he wondered if he might have found someone he could develop. He arranged a match for Charlie, who once again easily pinned a more experienced opponent. After that Charlie bought a booklet describing wrestling holds and joined the Swedish athletic club to be around people who could help him develop his skills.

Charlie entered the Central Amateur Athletic Union championship in Chicago in 1924, winning gold medals for both middleweight and light heavyweight amateur championships.[21] Following this win the young man from rural Wisconsin earned a spot in the National Olympic Trials at Madison Square Garden in New York. Contenders competed for a place on the US wrestling team for the 1924 Olympic Games at Paris, France.[22] Charlie won the 158-pound class, but the result was not binding. Officials for the US team decided not to take a chance on the diminutive, relatively unknown Charlie Fischer to represent his country. Charlie's name did not appear on the final roster, and he was denied the opportunity to participate in the Olympics that inspired the movie *Chariots of Fire*.[23]

In 1925 Charlie, now five-foot-three and wrestling as "The Little Demon," began his professional career. Charlie's most dangerous move was the Pile Driver. He would pick up a much larger opponent and drive his head into the mat. "The Pile Driver was sudden and deadly," wrote Ken Boness, Fischer's biographer. "No one spoke of Fischer's pet hold as unbreakable, as it only lasted a few seconds; almost as soon as it was applied it was released. And, caught in a pile driver, the victim had no contact with the mat until Fischer allowed it. By then it was too late."[24]

Charlie's wrestling career drew to a close in 1937, after participating in more than one thousand wrestling matches in thirteen years. He retired as the undefeated middle and light heavyweight wrestling champion.[25] A year earlier he had begun to build his resort at Bear Lake, where he owned one thousand acres of forested land.[26] In 1947 the Butternut School District adopted the name "Midgets" in Fischer's honor and continues to use the team name long after Fischer's passing on November 16, 1982, at the age of eighty-four.[27]

We located the river exit, flowing through tall grass, and pushed our way through into the flowing river. Twilight had set in, and we started to wonder if we would be sleeping in our canoe. What sort of situation was I putting my daughter in? At the very least we would have an adventure.

We met a man and a young boy fishing out of a rowboat. The man told us that all of this land is either private or swamp down to County Highway GG, but he was able to point us to an island below a small set of rapids about a half mile down, near the site of an old Civilian Conservation Corps camp. We paddled hard, through the last glimmer of day and into the gathering moonlight. Slivers of pink clouds reflected on the surface of the river.

When I heard the small rapids, I got out of the canoe, grabbed a rope, and prepared to guide us through the rocks. Water swirled around my legs as I picked my way through. My daughter sat in front, bracing herself with both hands on the bow. At the end of the rapids the canoe dipped, and what seemed like a million mayflies surrounded her. KC shielded her eyes with her hands. I imagined her covered in fairy dust, though she doesn't remember it that way. I felt the canoe push gently into the upper edge of the island. KC got out, managing to escape the bothersome mayfly swarm, and steadied the boat as I pushed us into shore.

We explored the island under the sliver of moon and chose the lower end to pitch our camp. We stomped down the grass and erected our tent. KC climbed into her sleeping bag and immediately fell asleep. I opened a small bottle of wine, looked up at the stars, and listened to water babbling by. An umbrella of stars hung over our campsite, and the river provided a small symphony, the high sounds over the rocks close to our tent mingling with the deeper bass sound farther downstream. Later, in my sleeping bag, I listened to my exhausted daughter breathe deeply in her sleep; an occasional deer splashed across the river below our tent.

The following morning, KC and I would continue our journey on the East Fork before returning to our regular lives until our next leg of the journey resumed. Our intermittent river excursions continued in this way for the next thirteen years, taking us the entire length of the river. While our travels often brought us into contact with people such as Matt and Robert Hart and the kind fisherman who helped us find a campsite that night, over time I realized how much of the story of the river happens off the water—in the communities that grew up around it, sometimes depending on the water, sometimes merely coexisting with it. I wanted to tell the stories of the residents of the Chippewa River Valley, why they stayed or why they felt themselves drawn back to the water. With this in mind, I returned to Glidden some years later with my son Andrew to begin again—this time with the goal of getting to know the towns and people along the Chippewa.

CHAPTER THREE

Beyond the Water

Return to Glidden

And I knew what hope it was. It was just that kind the place
was meant to encourage, that a harmless life could be lived
here unmolested. To play catch of an evening, to smell the
river, to hear the train pass. These little towns were once the
bold ramparts meant to shelter just such peace.

—MARILYNNE ROBINSON, *GILEAD*

On January 9, 2009, after a five-hour drive from St. Paul, Drew and I arrived at Roxy's Bar in Glidden. I asked the bartender, a blond woman in her thirties, if the newspaper was still in business. She brought me several back issues and said, "It's your lucky day. The man who holds it all together is playing one of those electronic games against the wall."

Pat Bonney had overheard our conversation. He greeted us with a friendly grin, happy to hear about my previous visit, years earlier, to find where the river starts.

"That wasn't the source," he said, grinning. "You can't canoe to the source. The source is a pool. You can see it from the road. It flows underground for a while to near the place you were."[1]

Pat worked for the *Glidden Enterprise,* one of the oldest

family-owned newspapers in Wisconsin, founded in 1903 and originally published in German. When I told him I was a writer and filmmaker, he asked if I would like to read some of his own work. When I said I would, he left and returned with two large three-ring binders full of his columns—providing plenty of background material for me as I set out to know the town better. Pat suggested the local motel to us, and we checked in there, agreeing to meet the next morning at the *Enterprise* office for a chat and a filmed interview. I was going to document my trip downriver through writing and a series of short films. In the meantime, Andrew and I set out to explore. First we visited the office of the US Forest Service a short way out of town on Highway 13. The wall just inside the door hosted a display of mounted fish and small animals, descendants of the oldest river residents. I browsed a rack of brochures, one of which described ongoing attempts to develop an elk herd nearby. It caught my attention because we'd passed signs on the way into town indicating we were in an "elk area" and advising us to slow down to forty-five miles per hour if the light was blinking.

The woman at the front desk asked us how she could help. I stood speechless for an embarrassing split second—not knowing quite what I was looking for—but my son Drew came to the rescue, striking up a conversation about the elk. After the woman explained that the flashing light indicated an elk was somewhere within a mile and a half, I mentioned my interest in how the local forests relate to the Chippewa River, hoping my vague inquiry would lead her to answer questions I didn't know how to ask.

She retrieved some maps printed on pink and blue typing paper, coded for the East and West Forks of the Chippewa. "Wait a minute. I'll get someone for you," she said, then disappeared back into the office area. After a moment, a trim, middle-aged man wearing a forest service outfit appeared. His responses, supported later by additional research, allowed me to develop an adequate, if rudimentary, understanding of the history of the area's forestland and of how its health affects the local watershed.

After the US government acquired the land from the Ojibwe via the treaty of 1837, businessman Ezra Cornell purchased nearly half a million acres of it as an investment under the Land-Grant College Act, also known as the Morrill Act. The purpose of the act was to use revenue from the pine lands for the purpose of establishing universities. Cornell purchased land for sixty cents an acre, later selling it for more than twenty dollars an acre to lumber companies. He used the profits from the sale to fund the opening of Cornell University in Ithaca, New York.

The 840,000-acre Chequamegon National Forest was created in the 1930s following the end of the logging era, as one chapter of a national forest movement that began in 1905. The logging companies had left a landscape of high stumps and brush piles ripe for fires; the introduction of government forest management saved the regional economy and restored the river. Research on logging in Europe had revealed that as the trees disappeared, the rivers shrank because of increased erosion and the effects on the water cycle of decreased shade, and such was the case with the Chippewa.[2]

Glidden lies at the western edge of the Chequamegon National Forest and houses the ranger offices for the largest of several districts, with 214,000 acres. As visitors enter Glidden today from Park Falls on Highway 13, they will probably see a huge pile of logs on the left side of the highway. The US Forest Service licensed the cutting of this timber. This is pulpwood waiting to be hauled to Cloquet, Minnesota, to be made into cellulose pulp, which is used in the manufacture of textiles. Over the years the fragile economy of the town has been sustained by wood: sawmills, charcoal kilns, and factories making everything from veneer and wood shingles to broom handles, cheese boxes, and fire starters. In 2008, Black Bear Forest Products closed, and the same year the local school district merged with Park Falls, home of the Flambeau River Papers Mill, where many Glidden residents have found work. When we'd completed our chat with the forest ranger and his receptionist, we took the pink and blue maps and headed out, eager to see more of the region we'd been learning so much about—and maybe even an elk.

A few miles southwest of Glidden, we passed a field of large round hay bales gathering snow in the fading light. In the early days of Glidden, many Germans immigrated to the area in hopes of starting a successful farm. Most would learn that the land suited to the white pine was not ideal for agriculture. This was one of the few areas of tillable land we saw in the area.[3]

A light snow was falling as we drove toward Shanagolden on the East Fork of the Chippewa. A colorful boulder marks the turnoff on Highway 13, a few miles northwest of Glidden. With a population of just 125 according to the 2010 census, this tiny town once held much loftier aspirations. The Shanagolden story is the stuff of romantic logging legend, though now all that remains of the operation are stone foundations in the tall grass along the Chippewa.[4]

The story begins in 1901 when Tom Nash, president of Nekoosa Lumber Mill in Grand Rapids (now Wisconsin Rapids), decided to build a mill along the Chippewa in a picturesque area a few miles south of Glidden. He enlisted the help of his two sons, Guy and Jim, and William F. Vilas, a wealthy friend from Madison. They bought forty thousand acres in the vicinity of the village of Butternut for harvesting timber and located the mill on the outskirts of Glidden, near where the Chippewa makes a horseshoe curve. Named Shanagolden after the Nash ancestral home in County Limerick, Ireland, the plant would use the same sulfite process the Nashes were using to make paper at their Nekoosa plant.

Initially Tom's sons were in charge of the operation. Guy and Jim Nash built a sawmill, a planing mill, and a shingle mill, recruited some workers, and even laid out a plan for the town before running out of cash. Vilas bailed out the operation, but Jim lost confidence in the dream and returned to Grand Rapids, leaving Guy as sole manager. As a young man whose main interests were writing, hunting, and fishing, Guy was probably more attracted to the possibilities of an outdoor life along the Chippewa than the daily headaches of running a paper mill. In 1903 he married Florence "Floy" Philleo, an accomplished pianist and socialite in Grand Rapids, and built her a lavish house that he named House in the Woods to lure her to Shanagolden. They had two children, Tom and Jean, while living there.

But Floy found her remote life along the Chippewa less than ideal. Asked by a local resident if she could name a place she would rather be, she replied, "I certainly can. Right on the corner of State Street and Madison in Chicago."[5] She traveled back and forth between Shanagolden and Grand Rapids to visit friends or care for ill relatives. While she and Guy were often apart, their frequent letters show a continued fondness for each other. In 1906, when Floy entered a health resort for "nervous temperament" marked by debilitating headaches, she wrote apologetically to her husband: "I can imagine how desolate and cold the house is without fire or fresh air. Never mind. I'll be home soon."[6] His wife's overwhelming discontent was the first of Nash's high hopes to be dashed.

The mill grew to employ 250 men by the winter of 1905, with another 600 engaged in logging. Unlike other mills whose employees lived in tenant towns of rustic shacks, Nash Lumber Company assisted its workers in building decent houses, for rent or purchase with affordable monthly payments. As the community grew, it gained a post office, a store, a school, and a community center, as well as railroad track connecting it to Glidden. As Shanagolden came into its own, residents applied to separate from Glidden to be free of the other town's taxes. The township was made official by an act of the Wisconsin legislature in 1907.

But what appeared promising from the outside was already starting to decay from within. By 1904, Vilas had spent more than $250,000 to keep the mills afloat, and he decided against putting any money into the sulfite process that Tom Nash had once hoped to bring to Shanagolden. Vilas, concerned about the company's accounting practices, feared the area didn't have enough trees in the vicinity to justify the long-term investment. With profits slow to materialize and continued concerns about Guy Nash's management, the operation was restructured, becoming part of the Port Edwards Company.

The infusion of stability was short-lived. A devastating fire on a windy day in 1907 destroyed the main mill in a mere twenty-five minutes. Plans to rebuild never came to pass, and most of the workforce was laid off. In 1908, Guy Nash gave up his management role and his beloved House in the Woods to move his family back to Grand Rapids. For several years, he continued to visit Shanagolden, the town he had helped bring into existence, to check on the pulpwood inventory or even just to attend a town dance. Within a few years, he took over the Jackson Milling Company at Stevens Point, which also failed. After serving two years in World War I as a captain of field artillery, he returned from the war and lost one hundred thousand dollars in a cranberry operation near Wisconsin Rapids. Years later he wrote to a friend of the heartbreak he still felt over the dreams that never came to pass at Shanagolden.

In the Nashes' absence, Shanagolden persevered for just a few more years before succumbing to its destiny as a ghost town. In 1909 Port Edwards sold its lumber rights to the Mellon Lumber Company, and in 1910 it put the buildings of the town up for sale. Unable to find a buyer, Port Edwards closed the mill operation, effectively shutting down the whole town. In 1912 the Shanagolden post office was closed, and in 1914 six houses from the main street were moved to Glidden. They can be seen today on Park Street leading to Marion Park.

In 1925 Guy Nash's once-treasured but long-unoccupied House in the Woods burned, and soon the remaining cutover land was absorbed into the Chequamegon National Forest. Today the Shanagolden town hall stands as a memory of what historian Dave Engel called "an industrial romance."[7] A large patch of marsh grass along the Chippewa obscures the foundation of the old failed mill operation.

~

At suppertime, we drove to Gregg's Steak House, which later became the Glidd Inn, at the corner of Highways 77 and 13. The dining room was empty, so we sat at the bar, while a couple in their sixties sat at the other end finishing their hamburgers and drinking beer out of bottles. The man wore a cowboy hat; the woman had a tired face and a nervous look in her eyes. The bartender told me that earlier that night a car coming in on Highway 77 had skidded through the intersection with Highway 13 and ended up in his front yard. He and some friends had helped the owner dig out the car, at which point the man drove off without thanking them. Over dinner, I tried my best to be a different kind of out-of-towner. By the time Drew and I left, the place was filling up with regulars who'd stopped in to catch up on the latest local gossip.

The next morning Drew and I had breakfast at the Bruin Restaurant, a newly painted, white, two-story building on the corner of Highway 13 and Grant Street. The legendary "world's largest black bear" in its suspended death growl peers out from a glass case between the restaurant and the VFW building next door. A sign gives its weight, who shot it, and who found it—a curious distinction. As far as I know, the claim still stands, but it's hard to say for how much longer. The September 30, 2009, issue of the *Enterprise* reported that a bear killed—or as they say, "harvested"—in the Tripoli area came in dressed at 660 pounds, just 5 pounds less than the Glidden record holder. The article concluded, "Records are made to be broken, but our bear was taken in 1963, forty-six years ago. With the large bear population now days; one would say it is just a matter of time."

The Bruin boasts an outstanding omelet, which I ate while studying a mural of the old town that spans an entire wall. The painting, by Brian Long, depicts Grant Street as it was in the 1800s. A row of wooden buildings lines the unpaved street, sweeping gracefully up a long hill to the water tower. People stand in small groups, idly chatting. In the middle, three men are holding glasses. When I asked about them, restaurant owner Karen Powell laughed: "We don't know what they're drinking." In the lower right corner is the former name of the town: Chippewa Crossing. "That was our name back then," Karen explained. While the post office and maps use the name of Glidden, the unincorporated town is officially inside the Town of Jacobs.

Karen has created a place that's part restaurant and part history display. On the front counter, you can study photos of Karen's father and other classic Glidden characters such as Charlie Fischer, the 1930s wrestler who once owned most of the shoreline around Bear Lake, where the Chippewa widens a few miles downstream. An American flag hangs on the wall next to the door between the dining area and the lunch counter. It flew over Iraq, where Karen's son served in the military, and later covered the coffin of Karen's husband. They had once shared a dream of owning this place and bought the building and remodeled it before he died. A plaque next to the flag honors her son, an air force officer who has been to Iraq a number of times. Karen confessed she was fearful that he would be sent to Afghanistan. "I told my son to tell his superiors that your mother doesn't want you to go," she said with a laugh. As of our meeting, her son was working for the air force in Minnesota.

Karen Powell, owner of the Bruin Restaurant. RICHARD D. CORNELL

Glidden's pride in its military vets can be seen elsewhere in the town, on several outdoor murals that depict local veterans along with their names and years of history. This was the brainchild of Karen Thorp, who worked with Kelley Meredith, an artist from nearby Butternut, to paint the walls. For a fee families could have their loved one depicted on the wall; a star cost less. The walls now feature close to two hundred stars and portraits, including one of Karen Thorp's father, Alvin Zach. Karen gave Pat Bonney credit for the name—the Great Walls of Glidden.

After breakfast Drew and I headed for the newspaper office of the *Enterprise* to meet up again with Pat Bonney. The walls of the outer office were filled with photos, signs, certificates, bumper stickers, and handbills. I noticed a wooden plaque from the Wisconsin Newspaper Association recognizing Robert Hart, and a photo of a parade with five or six men in the lead carrying American

One of Glidden's Great Walls, a series of murals honoring local veterans.
RICHARD D. CORNELL

flags. An American flag tri-folded in a wooden case adorned one wall, next to a photo of two soldiers walking down a street.

Pat was seated on a stool in a room beyond the front office, going over material for "Days of Yore," the section of the newspaper that reports from the past decades. He gave us a tour of the front office, filling us in on some of the details associated with the memorabilia, then took us back to the room containing a Mergenthaler linotype machine, used for typesetting in the first half of the twentieth century; two Kluge small-job presses manufactured by Chandler and Prixe; and a large paper cutter—a museum of antiquated newspaper technology.

When Pat started writing for the paper, he was driving a school bus between Glidden and Clam Lake. In the thirteen years leading up to 2009, more than a hundred of his columns appeared in the *Enterprise*. In an emotional voice, Pat recalled the day when

Pat Bonney at work at the Glidden Enterprise. RICHARD D. CORNELL

he first asked the Hart brothers if they would consider publishing one of his columns. "They looked at each other, surprised, I think, about my request, and then said yes; I have been writing for the paper ever since."

I had had a chance to read some of Pat's columns the night before. The three-ringed binders he had loaned me contained about one hundred columns beginning in the early 1980s. Some recorded the events of the week; others were memories of town characters. In one, Pat wrote about his fondness and admiration for Dick Druschke, who along with his wife owned the town drug store and soda fountain from 1949 to 1989. Dick was known as a surrogate uncle for the local children, a warm, fun-loving man who made a store into a kids' hideout. In another column, Pat wrote from the imagined perspective of the "Oval," a classic build-ing in Marion Park on top of a hill overlooking the town, where it would be possible to witness the theft of treasured wooden horses from the local merry-go-round.

Pat's collection is a thoughtful reflection of life in Glidden, although he refuses to refer to himself as a reporter, and he's more likely to talk about town history than his own work. Sitting on a box of old lead type in the *Enterprise* office, he described his experience growing up in Glidden:

> I went to a Catholic school that was literally across the tracks on the other side of town. There was always a sense of difference between me and my Catholic friends and the Protestant kids. In the winter, we would run our sleds down the hill across the river and down Main Street. The big event of the summer was when the girls would arrive from Chicago by train to go to their summer camps. There was a skating rink in town, and I had developed my skills enough to get the job of keying the skates on the girls. That was a very big deal. But then the town started to go downhill. The logging business dried up, stores on Main Street closed, and now we're about to lose our school to a merger.

Before Pat and I parted ways, I made plans to return again soon so that he could take me up to see the true source of the East Fork.

Over the years, I have returned several times to get to know the people of this one small town. Two of my favorite times to visit Glidden are the Fourth of July and Labor Day, when small-town hospitality is at its high point. Hundreds of former residents return for the Labor Day celebration, a community homecoming featuring cookouts with friends, a baseball tournament at Matt Hart field, and numerous class reunions. On Sunday, in conjunction with a foot race on dry land, small rubber ducks race down the Chippewa River. Marion Park is filled with food stands sponsored by local churches, and the Glidden History Museum opens its doors. You have to walk into the park behind the pavilion to find the history museum, located next to the carefully preserved carousel that's operated only on special occasions.

The museum, under the care of director Frank Kempf, offers a memory lane of outdated technology, from old typewriters and logging equipment to a display of items you'd be likely to find in a one-room school a hundred years ago; a seventy-year-old flush toilet and a colorful display of Glidden High School memorabilia from periods when students were known as the Orioles, the Vikings, and the Bears (this place is too fascinating for one mascot).

One summer day while attending a fund-raising picnic in Marion Park for the ambulance service, I had the good fortune to meet and interview Bernie Peterhansel, who passed away a few months later. Then in his eighties, Bernie sat in the passenger seat of a blue Ford pickup wearing a Chicago Cubs hat. He told me about how he prayed in a foxhole during the Battle of the Bulge that God would get him back to Glidden. But things had changed, he lamented. "If you had deer meat, all your friends had deer meat. It's not like that today."

Many older residents such as Pat Bonney and Bernie Peterhansel wax nostalgic about the old Glidden—getting a malt at Druschke's soda fountain after a basketball game, greeting the girls who arrived from Chicago on the train to attend summer camp on Buffalo Lake, roller skating in Marion Park. But while Shanagolden faded away when its reason for existing passed, nothing of the sort has happened just upriver. If Glidden is a community in economic decline, it doesn't act like it. During my visits, I witnessed the community make improvements to a community center for the developmentally disabled, begin replacing the mural in front of the town hall, and start a fund-raising campaign for new historic-looking streetlights downtown. Residents organized a picnic to raise money for an ambulance, held a community Father's Day picnic, hosted the annual Memorial Day community fair, and created a community beautification committee. The town lost its school, but the Glidden kids made new friends in Park Falls and proudly re-emerged as the Screaming Eagles. And so it carries on, as many of the small river communities born during the logging industry have done.

~

CHAPTER FOUR

Where Waters and Cultures Meet

Lake Chippewa Flowage

You know how it is with a favorite place. You let it live and
breathe in your memory and you feed it with rainbows and
you decorate it with roses and you bring it out from time to
time to caress it. Then you put it away until you need it again.
—Jay Reed, Milwaukee Journal outdoors writer,
about Lake Chippewa

A cool, hazy day welcomed us as we crawled from our tent on
our little island on the East Fork. It was about 5:30 on an August
morning. KC explored the island as I prepared a breakfast of pan-
cakes and coffee, the first use of my camp stove. We packed up and
pushed off at 7:30. A rough river day awaited us, lots of rapids and
exposed rocks. It seemed like we spent half of our time dragging
the canoe through obstacles. The most frustrating experience was
to get hung up on a rock in calm water. We'd paddle along when
suddenly—*scrape!* There we would be, hung up until we waded
in to dislodge the canoe.

When we entered the channel of upper Blaisdell Lake, a stiff
wind out of the south-southwest came on us. Sometimes we paddled directly into it; sometimes it came from the side, pushing

KC resting in the canoe after paddling through the wind. RICHARD D. CORNELL

us. We dealt with the wind for the better part of an hour before spotting an access road where we could pull ashore. The canoe had taken on so much water that it had become difficult to maneuver. The landing was a gravel road that terminated at the lake, fronted by a row of large rocks. We had to unload the canoe and lift it over the obstacle. As we lunched on everything we could get our hands on—crackers, peanut butter, sausages—dark clouds appeared on the horizon. As we awaited the storm, KC sprawled out on the backseat of the canoe and fell fast asleep. After an hour, only a few sprinkles had materialized.

The weather continued to look ominous, so we walked up the road looking for a cabin, hoping some kind stranger would lend us their phone. We were lucky to find Joe and Rose Musavage, who took us in. From there, we called our friend Dennis Aney, who knew the place, and he picked us up. Although disappointed to end our trip so abruptly, we were grateful to find refuge from the impending storm.

Resuming our journey several weeks later, we booked a cabin at the East Fork Resort. It was located a short distance upriver from the Winter Dam, which would take us a day of paddling to reach. The motel owner drove us to the outlet of Blaisdell Lake. Immediately after paddling clear of the lake, we got hung up in the rocky rapids at the outflow. Two men working at a nearby cabin helped to free us, and we paddled on, soon reaching the long, angular, 113-acre Hunter Lake and then Barker Lake after that. Upon entering Barker Lake we paddled past the former home of gangster Joe Soltis. During the Prohibition era, the sometime rival and sometime associate of Al Capone controlled the beer business in southwest Chicago.[1] He built a two-story lodge here after retiring.

As we left Barker Lake, the Highway B Bridge came into view, and we heard the subtle roar of the Goose Eye rapids ahead. You often hear rapids before you really know what you're dealing with. This feeling of risk, of the unknown, is one of the attractions of canoeing. Our guidebook advised caution. We roped our canoe and guided it through the boulders without too much difficulty. We would not hear that raucous river song again until below the Winter Dam.

A few miles below the rapids we arrived at the resort and the Chippewa Flowage. The flowage is a fifteen-thousand-acre expanse that includes three rivers and several lakes, featuring several islands with campsites run by the Department of Natural Resources (DNR). The largely undeveloped shoreline is dotted with resorts, converted from old logging camps, which have been popular fishing destinations for the better part of the last century. As early as 1917, an Ojibwe named Billy DeBrot built a few cabins and started a fishing camp, drawing affluent visitors from southern Wisconsin and Illinois. By 1973 the flowage was surrounded by thirty-odd resorts and had become known as the musky fishing capital of the world. But the recreational focus that evolved here masks old injuries that run deep, just as the placid waters now cover remnants of the Ojibwe communities that predated it. Paddling through this enormous and labyrinthine reservoir, we thought of the sacred Ojibwe land that lay beneath.

∽

The Ojibwe arrived in these parts in 1745 to occupy an abandoned Odawa village, where they used the rivers to engage in trade with other Indian nations.[2] The Ojibwe's first known encounter with a white man occurred in 1766, when Jonathan Carver paddled up the Chippewa River from the Mississippi. It's also possible that some of the Lac Courte Oreilles (LCO) Ojibwe met Pierre-Esprit Radisson when he explored the area for furs in 1659. In the centuries following first contact, the enterprising Ojibwe engaged in trade with the Europeans, exchanging valuable furs for manufactured goods. Many also became active and employed in the growing logging industry. While these activities provided economic benefits in exchange for cultural trade-offs, the events of the twentieth century found the Ojibwe fighting to preserve their way of life.

In 1917, after the bulk of the region's white pines had been harvested and floated downstream, surveyors arrived on the LCO Reservation, located mostly in Sawyer County, to measure and calculate.[3] Rumors immediately began to circulate that the electric utility wanted to build a dam on the reservation a few miles southeast of the Village of Post, which got its name from the trading post that an entrepreneur named Thad Thayer built there in the 1870s to accommodate Ojibwe and white loggers alike. In its heyday, about 180 Ojibwe traders and French Canadians lived at Post. The village later marked the terminus of the Chippewa Trail that started in Chippewa Falls and ran north, mostly parallel to the river.

The rumors were well founded. Now that the river no longer served as the major route of transportation for the timber industry, Wisconsin's economic leaders saw it as a source of cheap hydroelectric power and a way to control the flow of the headwaters as they flowed downstream. Two dams had already been built on the river: the Dells Dam in Eau Claire in 1878, and a second, huge dam constructed in Wissota in 1917.[4] Ultimately six dams would corral the river from the Ojibwe reservation to Eau Claire. The most controversial was the Winter Dam affecting the Lac Courte Oreilles.

The treaty of 1854 that established the reservation had contained a provision that allocated eighty acres apiece to individual tribal members. By the early 1900s, many had sold their land to whites, and the power company had purchased some of the parcels. But the tribe still owned 525 acres that it refused to sell. The Wisconsin-Minnesota Light and Power Company, joined by other power companies that would benefit, went to Washington to lobby for the passage of the Water Power Act of 1920, which would negate the previously agreed-to treaty rights. The act passed, clearing the way for the dam with certain stipulations.[5] To compensate for the Ojibwe lands expected to be flooded by the dam, the power company stated that it would build a new village on the shore of the flowage that would include houses, store buildings, and a church and pledged to move affected Indian graves to a new upland cemetery. To replace lost food sources, they agreed to stock the flowage with muskellunge, pike, and bass, to replant the wild rice beds, and to pay for one year's crop in addition to paying a yearly rent of twelve hundred dollars for the lands to the tribe. But the power company failed to fulfill its promises.[6]

The language of the power company's lobbying efforts had been legalistic. By contrast, the response of the Ojibwe was one of eloquent fury, as captured by William Wolf of the LCO Tribal Council:

To put under water the sacred bones of our honorable fore-
fathers is outrageous. The prayer and desire of this band is to
be in the same bosom that shields the remains of our fathers,
whenever the time comes.[7]

Tribal leaders argued passionately to protect their land against
the power of Washington and the interests of the power company,
to no avail.

Over the furious objections of the Ojibwe, who were unwill-
ing to sacrifice important lands for the meager compensations
being offered, Winter Dam was built in 1923 by Wisconsin-
Minnesota Light and Power, which later became Northern States
Power (NSP) and finally Xcel Energy. The water that built up behind the dam flooded seven lakes—Crane, Scott, Chief, Desire,
Pokegama, Charles, and Pahquahwong—and three rivers. The
flooding destroyed Ojibwe villages and ruined their cranberry
bogs. Also devastated by the newly created reservoir were hundreds of acres of wild rice that held spiritual and economic significance for the Ojibwe. In addition to its nutritious value, wild
rice plays a key role in Ojibwe ceremonies and in its traditional
stories. According to traditional Ojibwe legend, Ojibwe ances-
tors came to rely on this staple after supernatural intervention. In
one version, a young Ojibwe man known as Wenabozhoo came
upon a field of wild rice, or manoomin, while on a spiritual fasting
journey. The manoomin spoke to him in a dream, with a message
he then carried back to his people about this new food source.
Other versions of the story give the man's name as Nanabozho, a
prominent character in tribal folklore.[8] Thus, the commercial and
spiritual value of the wild rice that was flooded out by the Winter
Dam is incalculable.

As water gathered, the tribal village of Post began to sink beneath it. Many Natives failed to fully grasp what was about to
happen to them. This observation was shared by Edwin Tainter

writing in the *Lac Courte Oreilles Journal*: "Some weren't even moved out yet, because they really didn't believe this was going to happen to them. I saw the men trying to get people moved out of their homes. You could see the heads of the horses sticking out of the water." Denny Reyes, manager of the Landing Resort, the only Ojibwe-owned resort on the flowage today, was overcome with emotion as he recalled seeing those images. "I know," he told me. "I have seen the pictures."[9]

As the water rose, the power company's commitment to its promises waned as it made a number of amendments to the project agreement. One relieved the power company of its obligation to restock the fish. Next the company decided against replanting wild rice, building new homes, or relocating approximately seven hundred graves. NSP, which had purchased the Wisconsin-Minnesota Light and Power Company, offered relatives twenty-five dollars to tend the graves left behind. Ojibwe families refused to accept the money, seeing it as grossly inadequate to compensate for the promises that had been reneged upon. Today a marker on the bank of the flowage at the Landing Resort on County Highway CC proclaims that the Ojibwe never agreed to the flooding of their land.

In the early 1970s the fifty-year federal license for the dam expired, and a renewal process began. At this time the tribe seized the opportunity to reassert its rights. Members of the American Indian Movement, commonly referred to as AIM, took over the dam, drawing the attention of the national media. "Recapture" became the rallying cry of a coalition of Ojibwe, environmentalists, and white allies to limit NSP's control of land around the flowage. They succeeded to an extent. The Wisconsin DNR purchased the NSP land and created a public management coalition. Beginning in 1988, these agencies met to develop a flowage management plan. Representatives of the tribe, the state DNR, and the US Forest Service wrote and continue to manage the

environmental plan. Xcel Energy remains an active and sup-
portive partner.

~

Dams have been around the valley as long as beavers. These industrious fellows have constructed thousands of dams in the feeder
streams and creeks to the Chippewa since time immemorial, and
humans followed in their industrious footsteps. An estimated 148
man-made dams sprang up on the river system during the height
of the logging era.[10] In 1905, Wisconsin Governor Robert M. La
Follette reflected on the influx of modern dams:

> Our navigable streams and rivers, like our streets and high-
> ways, are open to the free use of the people of the state. . . .
> I believe that the state should encourage the development
> of its natural resources, including its water power system, in
> so far as it may properly do so; but the obligation rests upon
> those charged with the responsibility and clothed with au-
> thority, to encourage this development under such conditions
> as will justify and fairly protect the public right in these great
> natural advantages.[11]

As unjust as the Ojibwe story is, it is repeated even today as
large dam projects around the world are flooding people out of
their sacred places. Where there is moving water, there is someone who seeks to capture its power. Economics tend to trump
individuals and communities, and hydropower has gained public
favor as the cleanest and most renewable power source available.
Dams also often create recreational space, as has happened at the
Chippewa's Holcombe Flowage and Lake Wissota, places I will
explore as we go downriver. But these advantages do not come
without environmental cost.

The balance is reassessed when the federal government

relicenses the dams every fifty years. In the 1980s I was hired by Xcel Energy to facilitate meetings by business, governmental, and environmental stakeholders, our goal being to reach an out-of-court agreement among the stakeholders to achieve relicensing by the Federal Energy Regulatory Commission. Xcel would go on to receive an environmental award for its efforts at maintaining a more constant flow from the dams. During these negotiations I asked a representative from the US Fish and Wildlife Service about how he dealt with the frustration of participating in the seemingly endless discussions. He said, "I'll feel a little better when I see the river run a little more free."

The story of the Ojibwe is central to the story of the flowage. As I continued my exploration of the area, I realized I needed a guide to help me understand their culture. It was time to go see Little Bird.

I learned of Dr. John "Little Bird" Anderson from an article in the *Sawyer County Gazette*. It reported that he had come to Winter Elementary School to teach the children about Ojibwe culture. Would he teach me? After local historian Charlie Rasmussen gave me the number, I called, introduced myself, and dropped Charlie's name.

Anderson, who had taught American Indian culture and history at several universities, agreed to see me on a Wednesday afternoon. He directed me south on Highway 63 from Hayward. His driveway was a short road leading to a house on the top of a hill. I was thirty minutes early, so I pulled to the side of the road and listened to WJOB, the public radio station broadcasting from the Lac Courte Oreilles Reservation. It was January 12, 2012, and they were reporting live from the Wisconsin legislature, which was debating a mining bill. A mining company wanted to dig near the Bad River and the Bad River Reservation. The bill failed later that year by one vote, but a reintroduced bill would pass the following year, allowing the mining company to create an open-pit mine south of Lake Superior. The hearings leading up to the bill's passage were all held in the southern part of the state, far away from where its impact would be felt. The bill permitted a degradation of Wisconsin environmental protection laws. The movement toward the mine was protested by the Ojibwe, who place respect for the land in the center of their values. Eventually the mining company decided not to proceed because the area was too wet, but the debate surrounding it reinforces how conflicts between American Indians and governmental or business interests continue into modern times.

I drove to the top of the hill to John's house, past what looked like a large white macramé dream catcher mounted on a pole. The one-story house was a round stone structure resembling a lighthouse on a hill.

I passed the welcome sign to the door, which opened to reveal a man with a distinguished-looking face. I took off my shoes in the entryway, which had a few wet spots. He motioned me in and pointed to a chair at a small white table, then sat down behind a large three-ring binder. Charlie had suggested that I bring a gift of tobacco, and I held the pack in my left hand as he had shown me. Such gifts play an important role in Ojibwe culture—the tobacco signals a request by the giver, and acceptance of the gift means the recipient intends to grant the request.[12] John accepted my offering with a handshake and then took the tobacco with a reverent pause. Every time I have offered tobacco to an Ojibwe since then, they have accepted it in much the same way. They don't just take it; they absorb the moment. John's wife, Ginny, is a poet, and John shared a touching poem she had written about

FACING: *Wisconsin artist Sara Balbin's portrait of John "Little Bird" Anderson, which appeared in her book* Spirit of the Ojibwe. SARA BALBIN

an elderly Ojibwe woman. It begins, "The two-legged whites call anything that is not orderly, wild; they called Indians wild. We believe that everything is connected and important to life."[13]

John is featured in *Spirit of the Ojibwe*, a book celebrating tribal elders. The story of each elder is accompanied by a portrait by Wisconsin artist Sara Balbin, who depicted John as a swirl of energy dancing in front of a wild blue background, his lined face gazing intently at an eagle feather. I couldn't describe him any better. He spoke with passion about his years leading the Lac Courte Oreilles Ojibwa Community College, where he served as its first president in 1982, and his commitment to its mission of combining the "wisdom and beauty of Ojibwe heritage with the knowledge and skill of modern technological society." My conversation with John told me much about his character and about the complicated work being done to hold onto Ojibwe heritage, with its emphasis on the traditional values of pride, courage, service, and honor, along with being active participants in American society.

John had to end our meeting after an hour to get to court, where two young women he had sponsored were graduating from a drug recovery program. He agreed to let me attend and also invited me to give a short talk about my project to the LEARN Commission that evening. Lac Courte Oreilles Education Advancement Resource Network, or LEARN, brings together educational leaders to discuss resources and opportunities for Native students. When I arrived early at the Sawyer County Courthouse, a group of young people were talking and laughing down the hall. I sat a respectful distance away and waited until John appeared. He carried a large, white, fluffy plush rabbit and a fuzzy brown bear along with a small circular drum with a red thunderbird symbol at the center. When he sat down next to me, he explained that he had brought the drum to chant an Indian prayer in court, if the judge would let him. "You never know which judge you will get. Some won't permit it," he whispered.

We stood as the judge entered. He began by reminding everyone to stay for the whole session, saying, "We are all in recovery together." The first person in the room whom he recognized had been drug free for ninety-eight days. Speaking about the importance of total surrender to a high power, the judge asked the man if he had achieved that.

"Almost," the man said.

The next recoveree had been clean for seventy-eight days and had found work repairing pools and hot tubs. Asked if he felt gratitude for his new life, the man said he did—for the strength provided by his mother and friends and for the job that had given him new purpose. Another recovering addict spoke about the challenges and triggers in his life.

When it came time for graduation, the judge came down from his bench and gave diplomas to the two women John had mentored for their completion of the program. John walked to the front, offering his own experience with alcoholism as an inspiring example. "My name is John Anderson," he said, "and I am in recovery." He presented each of the girls with a toy animal and sang an Indian prayer to the beat of his drum, as the two young women watched solemnly. Some older family members were there with their disposable cameras, photographing the graduates with the judge and with John. I felt privileged to witness what would hopefully mark a turning point in these young people's lives, and came away impressed by their commitment to recovery and by the judge's show of support.

Shortly after my meeting with John, I was able to interview Gordon Thayer, chair of the LCO Tribal Council, who provided me with more insight into Ojibwe life on the flowage. In his Minneapolis office at the First Nations Recovery Center, which he founded in 2007, he told me that he was born in Eau Claire on March 14, 1945, and spent much time on the reservation. He recalled a night deer-hunting trip with his father when he was eight,

Gordon Thayer, who served on the Lac Courte Oreilles Tribal Council for fifteen years and chaired it for six. RICHARD D. CORNELL

in the early 1950s. After rowing up the flowage from New Post to where it intersected the West Fork, they stopped for a break at Bow and Arrow Resort, owned by his grandparents. The site is near present-day Johnson's Resort located south of County Highway B. After their hunt, they rowed back with one or two dead deer in their boat.

Thayer recalled days with his grandmothers, one of whom spoke only Ojibwe. He would sit with them and listen to them laugh and talk. "I knew Ojibwe in those days, but sadly lost it because of disuse," he confessed. On some days he would accompany one of his grandmothers, who hired out as a soybean picker. "We were poor," he said, "but just didn't know it." The house had no electricity, and all the cooking was done on a woodstove, something he remembers fondly. "Oh, how I would like to get my hands on one of those stoves."

When he was a teen, his parents moved him to Milwaukee, where he got into trouble with the law. Given a choice between reform school and the air force, he ended up serving two tours of duty in Vietnam in the Pararescue Unit. Pararescue is an elite branch of the air force whose members receive special training to conduct difficult and dangerous rescue and recovery missions, with similarly vigorous entry requirements to the Navy Seals. He was honorably discharged in 1970. For his service, Gordon received the Silver Star, Distinguished Flying Cross with Oak Leaf Cluster, the Air Medal, Air Force Commendation Medal, Vietnam Service Medal, and other meritorious awards. Perhaps more valuable, the experience taught Gordon that anything could be accomplished with vision and determination.

This belief shaped Gordon's work as chair of the Ojibwe Tribal Council following his election in 2011. Feeling that governmental economic-opportunity policies over the years had created a sense of dependency in the tribe, he adopted the philosophy "Mission Possible." This vision statement called for a reawakening of the roots of self-determination that lie deep in the soul of the tribe. He knew he would have to overcome the resistance of "naysayers and ankle biters," but with determination, he believed the tribe would rise to a new age.

In his role as tribal leader, Thayer also fought hard for environmental protections, upholding the tribe's long-held commitment to the land. After Thayer addressed the Wisconsin legislature on April 9, 2013, the Associated Press reported, "A Chippewa leader took Wisconsin officials to task . . . in the annual State of the Tribes address, accusing them of spreading 'propaganda' in a dispute over fishing, harming the state's natural resources with legislation easing the mining permit process and failing to give the tribes enough credit."[14]

"We can't be dismissed as a subgroup of people in Wisconsin," Gordon told me when we talked in 2012. "That's all I'm saying.

We're here."[15] Gordon lost the tribal head election in 2013 but remained on the board.

~

In my research of the river, I relied on local papers and driving around to scan for evidence of regional culture. Many of the resources related to the flowage story—including the Wisconsin DNR office, the US Forest Service, Sawyer County Historical Society, Weiss Community Library, and the *Sawyer County Record*—are based in Hayward, located roughly twenty miles away from the flowage. When people who live around the flowage say they are "going to town," they mean Hayward. So even though the city is technically outside of the Chippewa River Valley, I found it to be inextricably connected to the river's story.

I had subscribed to the *Sawyer County Record*, where Terrell Boettcher is an omnipresent journalistic voice. He's all over the paper, writing stories, taking pictures; he was the guy to go to for the local scoop. I met Terrell in his office at the *Record*. He has a doughy face and the look of someone who knows more than he shares. He suggested I meet Andrea Marple Wittwer, daughter of revered local historian Eldon Marple, and historian John Dettloff.

After getting directions from her husband, Ron, a barber who cuts hair in one of the oldest buildings on Main Street, I tracked down Andrea at their old farmhouse several miles east of Main Street. I heard the dogs before I saw them as I walked to the door. As I unpacked my gear and looked around, I noticed a picture of a red knitted hat on her computer screen. "I'm knitting hats now," she said, "and I'm already getting orders." Andrea is an ordained Wesleyan minister serving a church some miles away. She is thin and friendly and reminds me of water. She has flow.

Andrea lives on the land her grandfather bought when he arrived in the area in the 1800s. He was headed for Kansas, but a real estate agent enticed him to look at this piece of property. What

Sawyer County historian Eldon Marple.
COURTESY OF ANDREA MARPLE WITTWER

he saw was some of the finest land he had ever encountered. The topsoil was very deep, but it was cutover land, so lots of clearing would be required. Andrea's grandfather bought all he could afford—more than two hundred acres. Andrea described all the work required to clear the land, including dynamiting stumps, but said it uncovered the most fertile soil in the valley.

Andrea's father, Eldon, returned to the farm in 1914 after graduating from Hayward High School and earning a degree in agriculture from the University of Wisconsin. He served in various capacities advancing agriculture education: as a project leader of the Civilian Conservation Corps, ag teacher at Winter High School, and forestry adviser to the Ojibwe. He worked as an agricultural agent in California, Burma, Germany, and China. In 1966 he returned to Hayward to retire but stayed busy, bringing the Sawyer County Historical Society back to life. He wrote more than two hundred pieces documenting the history of the Hayward Lakes area and also wrote for the *Visitor*, a local tourist magazine. Andrea carries on her father's legacy and gives historical presentations. The building of the Winter Dam caused great frustration to her: "Hearing the story from my dad, it was an 'oh my gosh' moment. What was the state thinking to take the land from all those people?"[16]

On a ridge about ten miles east of Hayward on County Highway B you can look down into the Chippewa River Valley. To the right is the LCO Casino, Lodge and Convention Center, and to the left, a large expanse of flatland. Adam Cahow, accompanying me as I continued to explore the Chippewa flowage, informed me that this flat area is rich soil created by glacial outwash. As we drove through the undulating hills from Hayward, Adam pointed out features that had been shaped by the glacier—small ice-block pools, drumlins, and areas of glacial drift. As we gazed into the valley, Adam said this was where the watersheds divided. Rain falling in front of us would flow into the Chippewa watershed, behind us into the St. Croix, although both eventually flow to the Mississippi. I took note of the wide expanses of forest, another aspect of the geography connected to the area's past.

Hayward's history is closely tied to the lumber era, and lumberjack contests were popular in old logging camps. An event that puts the spotlight on this tradition is the World Lumberjack Championship in Hayward. To get a feel for it, I contacted Diane McNamer, who manages the show. I had arranged an interview with her a month before the event in 2012. She operates out of a wooden shack behind one of the bleacher sections around the pond where the log rolling and sawing contests take place.

Arriving for my appointment, I walked into a thriving media center to find Diane was on the phone with a reporter arranging coverage. She put the phone down, and I could see she wished I wasn't there—understandably, it just wasn't a good time. Quickly, I told her about my Chippewa River project. "But this isn't the Chippewa. It's the Namekagon," she corrected me, referring to one of the Chippewa's tributaries. "I really don't have time to talk."

Since Diane was short on time, I didn't try to explain how the river's story extended well beyond the actual water, or where Hayward fit into that story. Instead, I asked one question. How did this get started? "Why, Tony Wise, of course," she told me. "He created this, the American Birkebeiner, and Telemark Lodge."

Although not in the Chippewa Valley, Tony Wise's story echoes down it. He put Hayward and the neighboring river valley on the map in terms of recreation. Wise returned from World War II with a dream that he would build the kind of ski chateau in Hayward that he had seen in Europe. In 1947, the Harvard graduate began a small ski operation near a place called Mount Telemark. In 1972 he added a convention center, which some folks quipped was larger than the mountain.[17] But the convention center became known for its ability to attract high-profile musicians to the small Wisconsin town. Wise's daughter Janie told me that renowned jazz pianist Count Basie once played at her birthday party. Cheryl Treland also remembered those days: "The Monkees and the Strawberry Alarm Clock—here in Hayward!" Perhaps Tony's most lasting contribution, though, was to create the first American Birkebeiner. Known today as the Birkie, the fifty-five-kilometer race from Cable to Hayward is advertised as America's largest cross-country ski marathon. When the fortieth Birkie took place in February 2013, thirteen thousand skiers participated.

Tony also spearheaded the founding of the Sawyer County Historical Society and the creation of Historyland, where visitors experienced an old-time logging camp and a re-created Chippewa Village. But his dreams exceeded his revenues, and in 1980 he lost control of Historyland and Telemark. He died in 1996. In Hayward today a Comfort Inn sits on the former Historyland site. And though Telemark declined, the World Lumberjack Championship, the American Birkebeiner, and the Sawyer County Historical Society live on. The economic impact of Wise's endeavors still pulse cash, visitors, and vitality into the upper Chippewa Valley.

Treeland Resorts has deep roots in the valley's soil. In the early 1900s, as the residents of Post were going on with their lives on the West Fork of the Chippewa in the pre-dam era, Billy DeBrot built a fishing camp on the river that catered to wealthy visitors from Chicago and southern Wisconsin. He purchased the construction materials from Oluf Treland, a Norwegian immigrant who had a farm and a sawmill upriver from Post. Over time, the fishing camp expanded, evolving into Treeland Resorts.

I first visited the resort on an early spring day when snow was still on the ground. Harold Treland was remodeling one of the cabins, his work filling it with the rich aroma of newly sawed wood. Pausing for a chat, he agreed to join me for an extended conversation later in the month. When I returned, we met on the porch of the resort's main lodge, and Harold enlightened me on how the resort has changed over the years:

> When I'm remodeling a cabin, I always think about the people who will be staying and benefiting from the improvements. Things are always changing. In the early days visitors would arrive with their own boat and outboard motor. Today they want these things provided. We now have about thirty fishing boats with motors and fifteen rental pontoon boats. We had microwaves in a few cabins. Now they all have microwaves. Each bedroom has its own bathroom. The way to satisfying customers is to keep the women happy. If the women are happy they will bring their families back. We know we have been successful when a newly married woman brings her husband and family back. We have customers who have been here for four generations.[18]

A few weeks later I had the opportunity of interviewing Harold's sister Cheryl, who told me more about the family history. Her grandfather Oluf emigrated from Norway in 1910. He began in Iowa, then migrated to Two Rivers, Minnesota. Moving to Hayward in 1914, the family packed their possessions and a horse named Prince in a railroad car. At the depot in Hayward the railroad workers were having trouble moving a rail car, and Oluf offered to lend Prince to help. The locals scoffed at his offer, so he took bets that Prince could do the job. Prince moved the car, and Oluf collected his bets. "So the first thing my grandfather did when he arrived in town was to collect money from them," Cheryl concluded with a laugh.

Oluf purchased land between Chief River and Moss Creek. He had hoped to farm but saw quickly that the land was not suited for crops. Logging was the center of the economy, so he built a

John Dettloff, Brenda Dettloff, and Phyllis DeBrot at Indian Trail Resort.
RICHARD D. CORNELL

sawmill and started a dairy operation. When Winter Dam was built, the water from the flowage lapped against his farm. After the flowage had settled in, people came and offered to buy shoreline property from Oluf, but he turned them down. "I guess Grandpa figured it meant the cows had a shorter distance to water," Cheryl explained.

In 1938, Oluf started Treeland's Cabins. Cheryl's father, Oscar, graduated from college, taught for a while, and then joined the air force. When he retired, he and his wife, Jonney, returned to the home place to run the resort, with the help of their eight kids. At that point they had six cabins. "We were our own work-force," Cheryl remembered. "Everything that had to be done we did." Over the years Cheryl and Harold expanded the business, and today in addition to the original resort, the family owns Oak Shores, Pat's Landing, and Timber Kove. But both Harold and Cheryl still think of themselves as farmers, in the sense that they make their living through hard work. The big difference, according to Cheryl, is that "unlike farmers, when we have a failure, the government isn't there to bail us out. We live it, we work it, we don't punch in, and we don't punch out." This emphasis on self-reliance seems typical of the local values.[19]

Following up on the suggestion of Terrell Boettcher of the *Sawyer County Record,* I reached out to local historian and author John Dettloff. I also hoped to meet with Phyllis DeBrot, a full-blooded Ojibwe in her late eighties and the oldest living person from the old town of Post. John put me in touch with Phyllis's daughter, who agreed to contact her mother for me. The *Record* informed me of a film on Aldo Leopold to be shown on Thursday night at the Park Theater in Hayward; I put that on my schedule.

This would be the last week of the season at Indian Trail Resort, and John's wife, Brenda, said I could stay in the bunkhouse for a very modest sum. I booked two nights. The resort, located on the flowage, sits on the boundary of the ancient village of Post looking out toward Church Island. Indian Trail is a hard-core fishing camp: no sandy beach, no lounge chairs in which to appreciate the water. Old nets and lures hang from the trees, and no-nonsense aluminum fishing boats bob next to the dock. The bunkhouse holds a succession of small, plain rooms, each with a single bed. The toilet is at the end of the hall. This place is designed for musky and walleye hunters.

A neon sign proclaiming Enjoy Hamms Beer hangs over the entrance to the bar. Step into the bar and you're surrounded by the past, with a vintage juke box, an electric bowling machine, and a lighted pinball machine winking away in the dim light. Bar stools with orange vinyl covers line the bar. Behind the bar is a musky chart where people list the size of the fish they caught.

John opened a door behind the bar to expose a wall of the original structure. This bar sits on the very edge of where Post used to be. John's book, *Three Record Muskies in His Day: The Life and Times of Louie Spray*, is on display on a rack nearby. It describes how Louie Spray landed the world's largest musky on the flowage on October 20, 1949. The fish weighed 69 pounds, 11 ounces. On the walls are large mounted fish, including a musky—smaller than the monster caught by Spray, but still impressive.

Life around the Chippewa Flowage is inexorably linked to the celebration of fish. Ice-fishing contests draw fishers in the winter, and the summer brings musky and walleye contests. Musky images abound and figure prominently in the nomenclature of the area's resorts: Big Musky, Tiger Musky, Musky Haven, and Musky Joe's, to name a few. Treeland Resorts hosts a walleye challenge, the Hayward Bass Club out of Famous Dave's on Round Lake has a bass tournament, and Hayward hosts Musky Festival complete with a Musky Queen. In the spring, Fishing Without Borders, supported by volunteers, provides an opportunity for the disabled to cast a line.

Denny Reyes at the Landing observed that trolling—when a fisher drags a lure behind a slow-moving boat—is not permitted on the flowage. "There are just too many fish." Arguments erupt from time to time between the DNR and the flowage stakeholders over stocking walleye. The DNR wanted natural-grown fish and was not stocking larger ones, so the flowage stakeholders took matters into their own hands and sponsored a fund to support their own stocking.

～

Hayward is a small town. One of its bigger structures is a huge plastic musky leaping above the National Fresh Water Fishing Hall of Fame. It's so large you can stand in its open mouth with plenty of room to spare. Emmett Brown Jr., executive director of the hall of fame, claims that it was the musky that built the roads and the schools in this part of the state. "The musky has mythical qualities," he told me, "large teeth, yellow eyes, and a frightening way of leaping out of the water."[20]

Emmett's affection for the West Fork of the Chippewa renewed my own interest. I had found its source but didn't think much about it after that. With Emmett's assistance I was able to visit many stretches of the West Fork along the forest roads. And during Musky Fest in June 2011, Bill Linder-Scholer joined me to explore it further.[21]

Bill had been with me in my early explorations of the East Fork. We began our new study of the West Fork at Chippewa Lake, which we reached via a forest service road running north off of State Highway 77. The lake, formed by glacial ice when the glacier melted fourteen thousand years ago, is surrounded by trees and appears to be entirely undeveloped. The heavily used boat landing suggests that it's a popular fishing spot. Our next stop was Day Lake Recreation Area, four miles to the east. A dam was constructed on the Chippewa River here in 1963 to create a lake habitat for plants and animals.

At the nearby town of Clam Lake, the still-tiny West Fork of the river flows beneath Highway 77. Bill and I stopped in at the home of David Frasch, a former work colleague of ours who lives south of town on the shore of Lower Clam Lake. With glasses of chardonnay in hand, we plunked ourselves down into comfortable chairs and chatted with Dave and his wife, Evie, as we looked out across the lake.

Dave told us about his involvement with the Northern Wisconsin Elk Reintroduction Project. When the project got under way in 1995, elk had not been sighted in the area since 1866. The Wisconsin DNR teamed up with the Rocky Mountain Elk Foundation to foster a new herd, and as of July 2012 154 elk were living in the area, each with a number rather than a name. "They

don't want us to get too attached to them," Dave said. In 2013, the
Ojibwe shot a few of the elk as a means of drawing attention to
their treaty rights. Gordon Thayer talked about the controversy
surrounding this act in his address to the Wisconsin legislature
that year.

After bidding good-bye to Dave and Evie, our next stop was
the rock dam outflow of the lake, where the West Fork flows
under Highway 77 and turns to the southwest. Emmett Brown
had directed me to Firelane 174, where we could view the river.
At that point gentle rapids flow over the rocks. A mile or so down
the road we visited the Teal River, a tributary formed by the com-
bined outflow of Lost Teal lakes.

At nearby Moose Lake water rushes out of the dam, creating
pleasant river music as it courses over the rocks below. As we
gazed downstream we saw an eagle perched on a bare branch
above the river. Eventually he fluffed his feathers, preened his
wings, and glided off out of sight around the bend downstream.

Our next access point was the newly constructed bridge on
Moose Lake Road off County Highway S. Two boys in green life
jackets laughed and played in the small rapids below the dam. The
West Fork at this point is much wider than the East Fork, which
flows a mere six miles away. In my conversation with John Dettloff, I found out this has always been true, even before the dam was
built. According to *Wisconsin's North Central Canoe Trails*, this
bridge, named Orange Bridge, was where the Ojibwe massacred a
large number of Dakota in 1795. In the Battle of the Horsefly, one
of many skirmishes between the two rival tribes as they fought
for territory and, often, retribution, a band of Ojibwe ambushed
two hundred Dakota as they canoed downriver. All but one of
the Dakota warriors were killed.[22]

Back at Indian Trail Resort, we set up a couple of chairs
so I could interview John and Brenda on camera. As we were
wrapping up, I found out that Phyllis, the other person I hoped

to talk to that week, had arrived. Phyllis was sitting on a small porch across the walk from the bunkhouse. Her intense eyes were framed by beautiful white hair. John asked if she would like to accompany us out to Church Island, which had been a large hill before the building of the dam flooded the area. John and Brenda had been married on the island many years before. While John ran to get the boat, Brenda took Phyllis's hand and led her down the stairs to the dock.

Out at Church Island, John and Phyllis talked about the old St. Anthony Catholic church that used to stand here—a cluster of white birch now delineates the foundation of the church. In the 1970s, John "Little Bird" Anderson's foster father contracted to have the church dismantled because of the degree of vandalism that was going on.[23] We saw the remaining gravestones of the church cemetery, which NSP had promised and failed to move prior to building the dam. Both Ojibwe and French Canadian loggers had been buried there. Phyllis identified one sunken rock structure as an old root cellar. In the time we spent on the water, we had motored over an ancient village now covered by the silent water.[24]

∽

Each year in July, the Lac Courte Oreilles band hosts an Honor the Earth Powwow to celebrate the repatriation of their land. I had hesitated to attend because it's said to attract ten thousand people, with limited parking, and I wondered if I would be intruding at an event meant for the Ojibwe. But I realized that my portrait of the area would be sorely incomplete without some account of the powwow.

I found a parking spot near the elementary school without difficulty, and at the ticket booth I was given the senior rate— free. Things were going well. I wandered the grounds watching the Ojibwe visitors in their beautiful traditional costumes, soon noticing that plenty of non-tribal members seemed to be in attendance, too. Drummers assembled in the middle of the dance circle pounded out their mesmerizing rhythms, as an appreciative audience watched the dancers and formed an outer circle. I took a few photos and recorded some of the songs with my camera.

I met a young man wearing a T-shirt with "Mission Possible" on it—the slogan coined by former Tribal Chairman Gordon C. Thayer. Thayer was instrumental in bringing a new spirit of entrepreneurialism to the reservation, as well as a renewed commitment to individual accountability. Tribal cranberry bogs and lumberyards, commercial enterprises and a casino, are obvious signs of the reservation's economic vitality.

The more I experienced the area, the more complex the history of the flowage seemed to become. Just as the area's many interconnected creeks, rivers, and lakes flow together into the Chippewa, the many stories of the Ojibwe people before and after the flood run up against those of the visitors, resort owners, fishermen, the world's largest musky, even a Chicago gangster here and there. Al Capone owned a stone home and four hundred acres on Pike Lake, southwest of the flowage. It had a long dock to receive floatplanes bringing whiskey in from Canada. Cheryl Treland's grandfather remembered doing business at his mill with the infamous gangster, whom he remembered as a sharp dresser and a nice man. A man with an entirely different claim to fame, Dave Anderson, an enrolled member of the Lac Courte Oreilles Band of the Ojibwe, started his Famous Dave's restaurant chain on the shores of Round Lake, just north of the flowage.

I can't think of the flowage without thinking of all the people from various walks of life who helped me to understand its history. This story is about Andrea Wittwer, who carries on her

FACING: *The Lac Courte Oreilles band's Honor the Earth powwow.*
RICHARD D. CORNELL

father's love of local history, and Cheryl and Harold Treland, who with their parents and siblings built a prosperous resort on the flowage. It's about Kris Mayberry, the Sawyer County town clerk who thinks deeply about everything; Denny Reyes, who manages the Landing Resort for the tribe; Kathy Moe of the US Forest Service, who sees the flowage as a mecca for wildlife; and Neal Kephart of the Wisconsin DNR, who continues the work of guiding the environmental issues. And it's about John and Brenda Dettloff, who own and care for Indian Trail Resort on the edge of the old town of Post, and Dr. John "Little Bird" Anderson, who has tended to the vitality of the Ojibwe culture through education and perseverance.

And then there are those like Jack O'Connell and his son Sean, who remember the flowage in much simpler terms, as a place of beauty and fond memories. On a hot August afternoon, Sean and Jack sat side by side on a couch in an enclosed porch outside their home in Eau Claire. Jack is one of my dearest and oldest friends, and I had often heard him talk about their families' annual summer vacation near Hayward. It wasn't until much later that I realized he had vacationed on the flowage.

Jack and his wife, Ellen, had taken Sean and their other son, Tim, to visit a small resort the last week in July for twenty years. The trips are well remembered for fishing together, swimming on the sandy beach, going up to the lodge to buy candy, or heading into Hayward to ride the go-karts. Over the years, the O'Connells became friends with other families who visited at the same time of year. Jack described his love for the pristine wilderness around the resort: "We took the small boat out to an island to fish and were surrounded by trees and water. There was not a house to be seen, though that has changed as many of the small mom-and-pop resorts have been sold to make way for large houses." Jack was tempted to purchase the cabin they rented annually but decided against it. Now what remains is a shared family memory.

"I'll never forget it," Sean said, with his father adding, "Maybe we'll take the boys back there someday for a pizza."[25]

Though I knew I would never understand this complex place as fully as the local inhabitants, its character shone forth more clearly as I listened to the elected officials, tribal members, resort owners, government stewards, and everyday people I encountered there. At times, when I drove County Road CC to photograph sunrise on the flowage, I felt myself drawn to it. I imagined the mist hanging over the water as a powerful spirit of those who cherished it beyond my understanding. But it was time to move downriver.

In a few months KC and my son Brian would carry our eighteen-foot red Mad River and a fifteen-foot green solo down the rocky bank below the Winter Dam. This would be the beginning of a two-day trip downriver to Exeland.

~

CHAPTER FIVE

Moving Water

Winter

We forget that the water cycle and the life cycle are one.
—JACQUES COUSTEAU, OCEANOGRAPHER

I arrived back at the Indian Trail bunkhouse after viewing the Aldo Leopold film at the Park Theater in Hayward; it was around 9:30 on a Thursday night. I had visited the LCO Casino on my way back, where business seemed sparse. A couple of blackjack tables were running, and a few people were at the slots. After losing ten dollars at the nickel slots, I ran through a heavy rain to my car and headed for Indian Trail, hungry for one of the little pizzas that John and Brenda served at their bar. Two cars were in the small parking area. The large white Chevy owned by the young man in the room next door was parked down next to the bunkhouse.

It was cold, and three lights swung in the wind out at the edge of the dark water. After retrieving my backpack from my car and making my way down the cement steps, I lay my pack next to the bunkhouse door and went down a couple more steps to the bar. It was disappointingly dark, already locked up for the night. Back at my car I retrieved a small container of yogurt and a spoon from the little blue cooler, grabbed the handles of my cameras, and lugged them to my room, stowing the equipment next to my bunkbed. To stave off the chill, I put on my heavy sweatpants and black sweatshirt and retrieved a pair of dry socks from my backpack. Then I sat on the edge of the bed and had my supper. When I finally slid into the blankets and pulled the light chain, I mentally reviewed the day while listening to the sound of wind blowing against the trees, cabins, and other fixtures around the resort.

When I awoke, it was only 4 a.m., and I lay in the dark for a while hoping for more sleep before driving into Winter for coffee. The next time I looked at the clock it was 7 a.m.—time for me to explore the next leg of my project.

The day was cool, gray, and misty, with wet, faded red and yellow leaves pasted on the road. As I passed over the bridge near the Landing Resort, I saw three men fishing in a boat. I had learned from Denny Reyes, manager of the Landing, that this bridge was located at the center of the pulsating collection of waters that make up the flowage. The two branches of the Chippewa flow through it, contained by the Winter Dam.

Back on County Road B, I passed the green sign of Treeland Resort inviting me to stop by for pizza and ice cream. I passed over the Chief River and arrived at the bridge of the West Fork of the Chippewa. Using my mileage meter, I determined the road distance between the West and East Forks—six miles.

While Winter is part of the flowage area, I had decided that the town warranted a separate study. It was just thirty or so miles from Hayward, but the cultural and economic distances were significant. Hayward is the center of the action in Sawyer County, filled with tourists and well-off cabin owners. In contrast, Winter is the heart of the county's more rural south, which has some of the same refrains on self-reliance and hard work, but less emphasis on recreation.

In this area, all roads and institutions extend from Winter: the *Sawyer County Gazette*, Chippewa Valley Bank, Harvest of Friends Food Pantry, and the school district. And of course, the Chippewa, which runs northwest of town.

This is also the area of the old Chippewa Trail. While the Chippewa State Trail officially begins farther south in Chippewa Falls, a remnant can be found here in Winter. It originated as an Indian path and was later used as a stagecoach route from Chippewa Falls to the Thayer trading post on the LCO Reservation, which is now underwater. Highway 40 runs along the trail today, passing Cornell, Bruce, Exeland, Radisson, Ojibwa, and the logging-era Hotel Belille.

Winter's main claim to fame is astronaut Jeff Williams, who graduated from Winter High School in 1976. Williams served in the US Army and was selected by NASA for its astronaut program in 2000. In 2008 he spent six months on the international space station and orbited the earth more than 2,800 times. He collected photos of his experience in space in a book *The Work of His Hands: A View of God's Creation*. His picture adorns a billboard at the edge of Winter, and the Winter Wonderland, a variety store, hosts a small museum where visitors can see his spacesuit, as well as many photos of him in the capsule, and purchase a copy of his book. A sign hanging over the exhibit proclaims "hometown hero"—every town seems to need one. Glidden has the largest black bear, the Chippewa Flowage has the world-record musky, and Winter has Jeff Williams.

I began my research by talking with three people about the area: Sue Johnston, owner and publisher of the *Sawyer County Gazette*; Dr. Penny Boileau, a Winter School District administrator; and James Genrich, the town chairman.

Sue Johnston was the new owner of the *Gazette* after a number of years as marketing manager with the *Sawyer County Record*, based in Hayward.[1] She dreamed of having a newspaper of her own, but initially the owners didn't want to sell. Later, while she was visiting the paper to sell ads for the Lumberjack Championship, they asked if she was still interested. She was and put together a financial package to swing the deal, then recruited her son Nick to move from Minneapolis to help her. He sat by her side during our interview, as she proudly described the gritty, do-it-yourself culture of the area. "When people hunt deer around here, they do it because they need the meat, and they have canning parties to prepare for the winter." The people in these parts know how to take care of themselves, according to Sue. "If the world ever goes to pot, this is the place to be."

The town chairman was someone who exemplified the gritty local values described by Johnston. I found Genrich at the town hall.[2] He was a Wisconsin State Patrol officer who left active duty after being struck by a car while issuing a ticket near Wisconsin Dells, then served as Governor Tommy Thompson's driver. After retiring from the force, he bought a home on Barber Lake near Winter. Not satisfied with fishing, he ran for town chairman and served three and a half years until his death in 2013. The role kept him busy leading town meetings and making sure the roads were plowed in winter and that the beaches were ready for summer. But he was most proud of the town's school. Under the leadership of Boileau (whom everyone knows as Dr. Penny), students won national awards in vocation skill competitions.

I met Dr. Penny in her office at the school, which services not only Winter but also several of the other small towns I'd visit along the Chippewa: Ojibwa, Radisson, Couderay, and Exeland.[3] She started her career as an elementary school teacher. Her current title is administrator for the approximately 330 K–12 students learning under this one roof. While small, the student body has a strong sense of community that helps students thrive as they advance through the grades, Dr. Penny explained. "It's not a big change to move to high school here because they have been interacting with high school students throughout their experience." She invited me to tour the school, beginning at the school garden where students were working. The garden features a colorful painted arbor and a brightly colored piano, which a young girl implored me to photograph. The tour continued past a library that was used by all students, and then we stopped by a welding class, where one of the students showed me a souped-up lawnmower he had been working on. In the media room I watched as a group edited a film on the school year, using the same editing software I use, and then we popped into the band room to listen to them warm up. On our way back to the administrator's office, we stopped in front of the wall of honor, which features photos of all graduates of Winter who have served in the military.

That tour was in 2011. In 2013, I read in the *Gazette* that Dr. Penny had moved on to a new job in a school system in southern Wisconsin. The following year, James Genrich passed away following a brief battle with cancer.

It's the same story I have found up and down the river: an old comrade who has moved on, a restaurant that has changed ownership, a community beautification project that has added color where there wasn't color before. The communities along the Chippewa are as constant as the water flowing through them: always familiar every time I check back in, but always changing in the details.

The Chippewa does not flow through Winter; the dam that carries its name is located a few miles northwest of town. The Wannigan Restaurant and Resort is on the bank of the river four miles below the dam. Named for the floating restaurant that used to supply the loggers, the Wannigan is now a popular gathering spot as well as the launch point for several rubber duck and canoe races that operate as community fund-raisers.

On a warm July day, I was on the west bank of the Chippewa as it flowed past the Wannigan slightly above Bishops Bridge. In that morning's *Gazette*, I had read about the duck race fund-raiser for the Harvest of Friends food bank and decided to drive up from St. Paul to check it out. Inside the Wannigan, the rubber ducks for the race were available for purchase at the end of the long, curved bar. After I purchased my duck, a blue one, no. 192, I wandered around the restaurant. After watching some boys play pool and listening to the local gossip—I overheard one woman say she was Tom Selleck's cousin and that he used to come to family reunions, but not since becoming famous—I went outside for the race.

I watched as hundreds of ducks, tiny spots of bright color, bounced on the water and headed for the finish line. I knew my duck was in there somewhere as the mass floated toward a cable stretched across the river. A number of boys and girls wading in waist-high water were stationed behind the cable with nets and scooped up the ducks as they crossed. They yelled out the first five winners. My no. 192 wasn't among them.

Someone once said that you can't put your hand in the same river twice. As I watched the Chippewa flow by on the day of the duck race, I remembered I had been here before—this same spot, but in a different time, so perhaps a different river.

My first visit was July 30, 1995. Brian, KC, and I put in below the Winter Dam to begin a two-day journey that would end at Highway D near Exeland. KC and I paddled our eighteen-foot red Mad River, and Brian took the deep green fourteen-foot solo canoe. Before launch, we set up camp at Ojibwa Park near the river, a few miles above the intersection of Highways 27 and 70. We launched below the dam after carrying our canoes around a fence sporting a Northern States Power No Trespassing sign. I

Brian, KC, and me below the Winter Dam. BRIAN CORNELL

disregarded it because I knew it was not a legal sign; the power company did not own access to the Chippewa.

After about fifteen minutes of paddling we arrived at a good fishing spot. It was a triangular bed of small and medium rocks that protruded into the river from the right bank. Brian and KC started fishing and I worked to untangle the line of my fly rod. On her fourth cast KC caught a small northern, which Brian helped her release. I finally got my line untangled and got in some casting experience. As we headed downriver again, the first eagle of the day appeared. On the trip to Ojibwa Park, we had five sightings. Each took off and headed downstream, so we were never sure how many different eagles we saw. One eagle launched from a branch on the edge of the river right in front of KC and me. Another one, or maybe the same one, nestled himself into a tall pine and watched us as we passed. Brian paddled under the tree and tried to photograph it. After three hours of paddling and playing, we reached the takeout point across from Ojibwa Park, where we had claimed campsite number one.

After retrieving Brian's car, we went out to Dix's Chalet east of Winter for dinner. When we returned to our camp, I had hoped we could have a chat around the campfire, but Brian vetoed that idea, as his allergies had taken hold. After we set up our tent KC and I walked across Highway 70 to look at the river. In the fading light, the water barely seemed to move. The flat surface was speckled with what we thought were mayflies. Lots of crawfish were swimming along the bank. Two large herons took off in front of us, and many ducks scooted on the river and took off; we guessed they were canvasbacks.

This was the first time just the three of us had done something together since we took Brian to Iowa State to look at their architecture program. They sure weren't kids anymore, and I could feel how the years had separated us, since I hadn't lived with them regularly when they were young.

We crawled into bed, and I found out that KC had collected record albums since she was ten. We lay in the dark recalling favorite lines from movies: *Parenthood* and *National Lampoon's Vacation*. Brian had us in stitches with his Clark Griswold lines. We recalled great Steve Martin material, and KC said she had all of his albums.

Through the course of that day I was treated to small stories of life without me. An older man named Carol who had befriended the kids collecting frogs with Brian and eating the legs. Brian scaring KC at night by grunting and dragging his foot across the floor. Brian driving his Malibu to Delavan to spend time with his future wife, Kari. KC thinking her mom was worried. These kids have endured much because of my life's struggles, but their mother did a great job while I lived my life and tried to figure things out.

In two weeks I would be on French soil standing in Bellegarde, France, where my father, Ira, had died. I was thirteen months old when he was killed and knew him through my mother's tears and anguish. If he had survived the war, I would have grown up the son of a Wisconsin storekeeper; he had been buying a country store in Utica when he was drafted. That store was his dream, and it died with him, surrounded by the rose fields of the Loire Valley. As an only son of an only son killed in war, I was granted his veteran's benefits, which financed my college education.

My quest to learn about him took me to Camp McCain near Greenwood, Mississippi, where he was trained as a combat engineer, and to France. While I didn't have the chance to know him in life, Ira has given me much from the grave. I felt his presence in my life while spending time with my own children.

Like the Chippewa, life keeps rolling along.

The next day, following breakfast at the Lakewood Café in Winter, we packed up and moved our car to the D bridge east of Exeland. We were on the water by 10:30. The sky was clear blue, the temperature in the high eighties, with a wind that became increasingly challenging as the day wore on.

Downstream from the Ojibwa Park campground the river flows under Highway G, then turns south and enters the Radisson Flowage. The wind gusted close to twenty miles an hour. At one point KC and I were blown to the shore. Brian paddled in the middle, plowing through the waves into the wind in his deep green solo canoe. After a while he paddled over to a small island, and we joined him. After he had a chance to rest from all that paddling, we set out again and finally reached a dam where the river seemed to disappear. What should have been the river below the dam were the remnants of the once treacherous Belille Falls, now a jumble of naked boulders impossible to walk through with our canoes. We pushed to the right bank to a gravel road that paralleled the river.

After carrying the canoes about a quarter mile down the road and sliding them down through the grassy stump-speckled bank, we thought our problem was solved. But after only five minutes of paddling, the boulders again consumed the river. The water spread out into many, many small streams among the boulders. We pushed, pulled, and grunted through a small opening, slipping on the irregular rocks that constituted the riverbed. I began to feel pain in my lower back, probably the result of carrying the big red canoe down the gravel road, or possibly from twisting as I attempted to keep my balance. I decided to head for the edge—to call it a shore would be an overstatement—where the rocks were dry and visible.

After what seemed to be a mile of this mess, we finally spotted what appeared to be actual moving water. The river had begun to assemble itself along the right bank. Four and a half hours later and several miles downstream, the Brunet River entered the Chippewa as a small stream just above the Highway D bridge. The Brunet flows from Winter Lake and in the logging days was a significant tributary. These days it's too small to navigate.

When the D bridge appeared, we returned to the Ojibwa Campground and lashed the canoes to the cars. I headed south on Highway 27, with Brian and KC following. They were returning to their home, while I was headed for France.

Over the years I often wondered how I got us into this mess. When I later returned to the area with Adam Cahow and Jerry Price, we arrived at the right bank where we had begun our portage years before. Adam pointed out that this was one of three small dams that created the flowage. Scouting further, we came to a dam on the far left and a canal leading to the Arpin Dam. Signs that I had not seen during our initial visit indicated a better route for canoe portaging—lesson learned.

❧

Summertime on this part of the river means canoe races. Unlike in Glidden, where some residents live near the river without much noticing it, the waters of the Chippewa are celebrated downstream. The Lake Chippewa Flowage abounds with various fishing contests and a steady stream of fishers. The towns along the river below the Winter Dam celebrate the river with canoe races and, in Exeland, Trout Fest. The first canoe race of the season is the Ojibwa Community Club race from Bishops Bridge to the G Bridge.

On August 11, 2012, I returned to the Wannigan to film that race. As I was organizing my gear, a half hour before registration, I heard someone yell, "It's broken loose and heading downstream!" The current was so strong, a branch had broken free and was quickly swept downriver.

This river was different from the one I saw the day of the duck race. At that time, the river had been low enough to allow the teens to stand with water barely up to their waist as they scooped up tiny plastic ducks at the finish line. Now the river was high and fast.

The Wannigan was closed, so I used my time to walk the bank and consider where I might film the start of the race. A couple of men were fishing in an aluminum boat in the middle of the river. Then I saw Greg Haberman, who owns the Wannigan. I commented that the river was really running.

"I turned it up from 7:30 to 9:30 so we would have water for the race," he said.

I wasn't sure what he meant. "Turned it up?"

"Yeah," he said, "but first I had to check with my boss."

This still wasn't making any sense to me. "Your boss?"

"Xcel Energy. They hired me to manage the dam."

Now it was becoming clear. The Winter Dam usually releases

Greg Haberman, owner of the Wannigan, also manages water flow at Winter Dam.
RICHARD D. CORNELL

water from the flowage at 270 cubic feet per second (CFS). Then the river flows freely until below Bruce, when the effect of the Holcombe Dam slows it. But Greg had increased the water flow for the race.

I walked away, shaking my head. Turn on the river!

During my work on the relicensing process for Xcel Energy, I visited each of the five dams that were up for relicensing (Holcombe, Jim Falls, Cornell, Wissota, and Eau Claire) and observed their operation. The main issue was minimum flow. Xcel Energy had been criticized for maximizing power generation. They would store a huge amount of water behind their dams and release it when they needed the electricity. This resulted in a rapid rise and fall of the river that affected water temperature and eroded

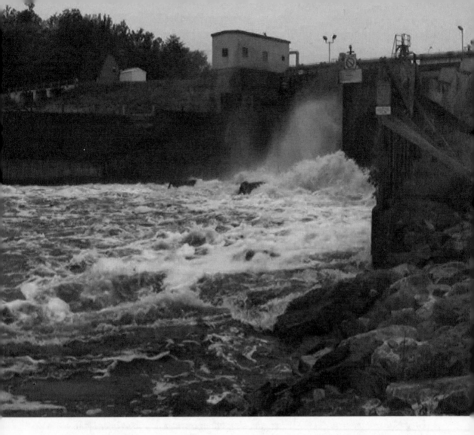

Winter Dam. RICHARD D. CORNELL

the banks. Also, by law the power company is required to have a canoe portage route at each dam. Xcel Energy claimed that because of the considerable investment it made in this producer of renewable, nonpolluting energy, the company had the right to maximize its profits. The environmental interests claimed, and were able to prove, that creating a large pool behind the dams and maximizing the flow through their generators created flux in the river that caused erosion and was detrimental to wildlife. A compromise was reached, and Xcel gave up a great deal of shoreline but retained the right to manage the water level on the flowage as long as it didn't go below 1,310 feet above sea level. A gauge above the dam records this level.

Greg's job with Xcel Energy is to operate the dam according

to specific parameters. The dam serves two masters. One is to maintain the Chippewa Flowage at the agreed-upon level. The other is to manage water as it flows downriver. When I talked to Greg in more detail at a later date, he told me about an early spring heat wave that rapidly melted the snow in the woods one year, causing the flowage to rise rapidly. He was asked to raise enough gates to release 7,200 CFS through the dam. "I didn't think I would survive it," he said.

I filmed the start of the canoe race from Bishops Bridge, then drove to the G Bridge to wait for the finishers. One of the first five finishers was a man in his eighties; he had to be helped from his canoe. As I was filming I heard the engine of an ATV. The driver, I discovered, was Tom Helsing. He stopped to talk, sharing that when he was young he played in the river with his friends. Tom had become a touchstone for me. I had visited his house twice so far. His father had been a Sawyer County game warden known for his ruthless enforcement of the law, and his grandfather had owned Helsing's bar on the corner of Highways 40 and 70 at Radisson. Tom recalled the first canoe race, which attracted a thousand people, including some Ojibwe who erected wigwams on the shore.

After a pleasant chat with Tom, I decided to move on, resisting the temptation to join the community picnic happening under a large tent. I had an hour before my scheduled interview with Blaire Shydlowski to talk about the food pantry.

On a previous trip to the area, Adam Cahow had directed me down Highway W to see a historical marker related to John Dietz, a farmer made famous for standing up to the logging industry. On Adam's recommendation, I had looked up the story in a book by historian Malcolm Rosholt. I intended to use the hour to see if I could find the historical marker. When I located it on the side of the road, a sign informed me that the famous Dietz Dam no longer existed but had once been located two miles south.

The conflict between Dietz and the loggers began in the early twentieth century. Dietz had recently moved to the area and began arguing with lumber corporate giant Frederick Weyerhaeuser over use of the dam on his property. He didn't exactly win, but his story is one of the most remarkable in the Chippewa River Valley, not to mention an early example of the locals' reputation for grit and pride. Dietz, who had been town clerk and treasurer in his hometown of Rice Lake, had been unsuccessful in the real estate business there. In a quest for a fresh start he took on the job of managing the Price Dam, owned by Chippewa Lumber and Boom (CLB), on the Brunet River and purchased a section of land a few miles from Winter.

Hugh Cameron, who had a lumbering operation, had previously owned the land, and Dietz, his wife, Hattie, and their six children moved into the old Cameron cabin located along the Thornapple River, a Chippewa tributary. While surveying his property, Dietz discovered that a dam owned by CLB on the Thornapple was half located on his property. He posted a No Trespassing sign on his side and demanded that CLB pay a toll to him for using the dam.

When someone from CLB arrived in the spring to open the dam to allow logs to float through on their journey down the Thornapple, Dietz pointed to his No Trespassing sign and claimed control of the dam. The man attempted to open the dam anyway, and Dietz fired a warning shot. William Irvine, manager of the CLB sawmill in Chippewa Falls, arrived to negotiate. He offered Dietz some additional land, but it did not assuage him. A warrant was issued at the Sawyer County Courthouse in Hayward demanding that Dietz open the dam. When the sheriff arrived to serve the warrant, Dietz shot at him as well. Thus began six attempts to force Dietz to succumb. But Dietz had a great deal of

John Dietz, pictured with his wife and children in 1906. WHI IMAGE ID 26626

local support, and the sheriff found it difficult to assemble a local posse against an ordinary guy who was standing up to a big corporation. Dietz had been effective at using the media to advance his image as a loner taking on Frederick Weyerhaeuser's giant Mississippi River company. Local law enforcement reached out once to Milwaukee and once to Chicago to recruit armed men for the job. Soon lawmen from those areas arrived to join the posse.

Meanwhile, thousands of feet of logs trapped behind the dam were in danger of rotting. In a desperate move, the sheriff decided to ambush Dietz on his weekly trip to Winter for supplies. On this particular day, a reporter from a Chicago paper delayed Dietz at home. His children went ahead without him and were on their way to Winter when the sheriff ambushed the wagon and started

Blaire Shydlowski, manager of the Harvest of Friends Food Pantry.
RICHARD D. CORNELL

shooting, one of his bullets hitting Dietz's daughter Mara. Seriously wounded, Mara was taken to Winter and then by train to Ashland. A settlement was reached with Dietz receiving pay from his work at the Price Dam in exchange for releasing half the logs from behind the dam. CLB moved their half of the load ten miles to the Flambeau, and Dietz sawed his half. The issue appeared to be settled.

Later, Dietz traveled to Winter to vote in the first election in Wisconsin. While there Dietz's son got into a fight with a local man over the rumor that Sawyer County would no longer supply a teacher to the Dietz children. The fight widened to involve John Dietz and another man. The other man knocked Dietz down, and Dietz pulled his pistol and shot the man in the shoulder.

The unrelated incident changed the dynamic. While the community had supported Dietz when he stood alone against big business, when he shot one of their own, he had crossed the line. A local posse, sixty strong, assembled to help the sheriff arrest Dietz. But Dietz didn't go down without a fight, and in the ensuing shootout he killed a sheriff's deputy and was wounded himself. His wife, Hattie, who was pregnant, lay on the floor of the cabin with the children during what became known in Wisconsin folklore as the Battle of Cameron Dam. Finally ready to surrender, Dietz sent his daughter Helen out with a white flag. When he stood trial for the murder of the deputy, Dietz served as his own lawyer. He was found guilty and sentenced to life, but the Wisconsin governor pardoned him in 1921. By this time Dietz had lost his property and had become estranged from his family. He moved to Milwaukee, where he gave paid lectures telling his story until his death in 1924.[4]

Following my visit to the Dietz marker I returned to Winter to meet with Blaire Shydlowski, a thin, vibrant woman in her early sixties. I had last seen Blaire at the duck race, when she was running about rounding up lifejackets for the kids who would stand behind the finish line. She had time that day to tell me she was coordinator of Harvest of Friends Food Pantry, and we agreed to have a longer talk when I returned to the area. We met in the food pantry located in the brick town hall off Main Street. It is likely this was the area where Dietz's Election Day gun battle took place more than a hundred years before.

Blaire, who once had a career as national sales manager for a large retailer, had followed her husband to Winter. She brought all that energy to her work for an animal shelter and frustrated her husband because of all the animals she brought home. When a need appeared to start the food shelf, Blaire stepped up as an unpaid volunteer. "When you get paid, it changes everything," she said.[5]

The food bank looks like a small grocery store with shelves filled with generic foods such as boxes simply labeled "cornflakes." Second Harvest, a Wisconsin hunger relief charity, supplies a great deal of the food, with the rest coming from donations and fund-raisers. The revenue from the duck race, a bit less than five hundred dollars, disappointed Blaire. The organization sponsors another large fund-raising challenge in the autumn, which she hoped would do better. But she has encountered resistance to their mission from members of local service organizations. "They think we are creating dependent people and that folks ought to learn to meet their own needs," Blaire said.

Blaire sees a difference in the giving attitude between the longer-term locals and newer residents. "Recent arrivals have come from larger cities and are accustomed to donating." The observation didn't surprise me based on my other encounters. *Gazette* owner Sue Johnston had described the independent nature of the locals, and Dr. Penny had shown me the school garden where children were learning how to grow their own food. The emphasis on self-reliance was a clear pattern.

I met another believer in self-reliance, Bimbo Gifford, when I returned to the river in the summer of 2013 to revisit the section that KC, Brian, and I had paddled eighteen years before. This time I was hoping to get someone who knew the area to accompany me, and Janet Gerber of Exeland knew just the person. "You have to talk with Bimbo," she said, without any hesitation. "Yes, that is his name." She said Bimbo had a jon boat that would be perfect for negotiating shallow, rocky water. I asked if my size would be a problem, as I could no longer handle a canoe. "Bimbo is a big man, too," she reassured me.

Chatting with Bimbo by phone, we arranged to meet to plan a possible river trip. I asked him about his fee. "Beer would be fine," he responded with a laugh. When I pulled into his log cabin on the shore of Windfall Lake east of Exeland, he was standing next to his jon boat. "The cooler has beer and water," he said, after shaking my hand. "Let's go." So much for the planning meeting.

We picked up Bimbo's longtime fishing partner Dean Johnson, who drove Bimbo's truck and boat trailer to Highway D. On the way we passed the old French cemetery that KC and I had visited years before. Bimbo backed his boat trailer to the river as though it were attached to the truck's bumper. We put in below the Arpin Dam at Radisson, where the river was flowing nicely. I asked him if the Arpin Dam determined the flow, but he said, "No, the Winter Dam is in charge." I learned later from Tony Schuster, retired Xcel manager, that the Arpin Dam operates by the flow of the river, not containing a flowage. Bimbo gently guided us downriver now and then cast a large yellow lure.

Bimbo designs and makes fishing poles and lures. One of his lures fetches fifty thousand sales a year. He once made a fishing pole for retired Green Bay Packers quarterback Brett Favre, with Packers colors, green and gold, and the inscription "Brett Favre, MVP." He received a thank-you letter from Favre, which he has stored in a safe.

As he told me about his business, Bimbo rowed the eighteen-foot jon boat, which he had purchased from the Wisconsin DNR for a hundred dollars. The DNR had used it for fish stocking until the bottom rotted out, but Bimbo restored it.

During our four-and-a-half-hour trip he caught two nice-size small mouth bass, which he tossed back. He entertained me with stories of growing up on the river with his grandparents and showed me the place where his grandparents had a cabin and the place where he used to swim with his brothers. I mentioned my

Drew and I ponder the source of the Couderay at Helsing's bar.
RICHARD D. CORNELL

interest in the Couderay River, and he showed me the spot where
the tributary flows into the Chippewa.

This was the place where Jonathan Carver, on June 20, 1766,
took a left turn from his upriver trip and left the Chippewa to go
upstream on the Couderay.[6] The Couderay brought him to Little
Lac Courte Oreilles, the larger Lac Courte Oreilles, and finally to
Windigo Lake, where he portaged to the Namekagon. Then the
White River took him to Lake Superior, where he could make
his way to what is now Grand Portage. Dr. Rick St. Germaine, an
LCO member, former tribal chairman, and educator, described
this route to me. St. Germaine told me that Carver likely had a
Native interpreter with him.

The Couderay River and how it fit into the ancient history of
the region had been of particular interest to me. My understanding increased when a librarian at the LCO Community College

gave me a small book of Ojibwe history. It contained an early 1900s map, provided by Dr. St. Germaine, showing the names of the Native families who lived along the river. For centuries, the Couderay had been an important source of fish, water, and transportation to these people.

After immersing myself in the local history, I wanted to visit the Couderay's source, which was near Billy Boy Dam. My son Drew, a trained geologist and expert map reader, joined me. We drove to the historical marker for French explorers Pierre-Esprit Radisson and Medart Chouart, Sieur des Groseilliers, on Highway 27/70 near Reservation Road. The marker claimed they had spent the winter of 1659 near that place with the Odawa. A small stream flowed nearby, under the Highway 27/70 bridge. We drove, studied our maps, and looked for the source of the river. After many dead ends, we gave up for the day and went in search of a few much-deserved beers at Helsing's bar, in the town of Radisson at the corner of Highways 40 and 27/70. Once owned by the grandfather of Tom Helsing, whom I had come to know up in Winter, the bar is owned these days by Robert Villiard.

Robert, who goes by Bob, is part French Canadian and part Ojibwe. He left a career in the woods as a logger for what he thought would be an easy life as a bar owner. But things have changed. Fewer deer hunters come to the area, and stricter alcohol laws have made business more difficult. As I sipped my drink, I described to Bob our struggle to find the source of the Couderay. "It's just down the highway," he said. "It flows past the marker for Radisson." Immediately, it made sense that Radisson and Groseilliers would have camped near the source. That small stream we had seen was the Couderay, and Billy Boy Dam was just upstream. Even more exciting was the possibility that Carver and Radisson could have camped in the same area, about a hundred years apart.

~

On my outing with Bimbo, we continued our float through the warm sunny day after passing the Couderay. The sky presented us with a panorama of fluffy white clouds. The river was lined with tall pines and high, waving grass. It was easy to imagine the river as it was more than a hundred years ago. As we approached a bridge, Bimbo pointed to a high left bank where Charlie Belille's stopping place had been.

Local historian Eldon Marple discovered an interview with Charles Belille, the first white settler in what is now Sawyer County, in the *Hayward School Journal* dated November 1899.[7] Belille was born in Bercier, Quebec, Canada, in the early 1800s. Working for the Hudson Fur Company, he made his way up the St. Lawrence River to La Pointe. After marrying an Ojibwe woman, Esther Crane, he moved to Chippewa Falls, arriving in the area in 1835 or 1836. There, he found a good place to build what would be a hotel serving loggers. He was listed in the 1850 Chippewa County census with a different wife, Laura, and three children. Following three years at the falls, the family traveled upriver in a birchbark canoe to a place near the mouth of the Couderay, where he built a house. In 1857, Laura died, and in 1860 he married another Ojibwe woman, Maggie Amsiwesay. It is uncertain how many wives he ended up having, but he had an estimated nineteen children. It was reported that he often went to Chippewa Falls to buy supplies. When this story arrives in Cornell, I will share evidence that he did business with another important figure on the Chippewa.

Back on the river with Bimbo, we passed a large island in the vicinity of the Chippewa River Crossing built in 1884. Frustrated by the difficulty of floating logs from Potato Lake south of Bruce to the Chippewa, Frederick Weyerhaeuser laid six miles of track connecting the two, creating the first logging railroad in northern Wisconsin. The line was abandoned in 1910.[8]

A small sign on the west side of Highway 40 about ten miles north of D marks another spot where a railroad brought logs to the river. At this site is also the former home of Phyllis Sanders, a writer and lover of history who has written four small books on the area. Phyllis served as a librarian in Exeland and as an elementary school teacher on the LCO Reservation. After she passed away, her husband, Bob, and son, Larry, have protected her legacy. Adam Cahow, Jerry Price, and I visited them in October 2013. They showed us the remains of the Exeland rail station and the indentations where the rails had once been. Bob told us that buzzards lived in the attic of the station, and one day while returning to his home, he looked back to see three following him. "That really got me to thinking," he said, alluding to the forward march of time and his own mortality.

Bimbo had alerted a friend of our arrival and he was waiting for us at the D bridge to take us back to Winter. We agreed that Bimbo would take me downriver to the town of Bruce in June of the next year, when I would be working on the next segment of this journey. I parted ways with Bimbo with the promise that we would return to the river the following summer.

CHAPTER SIX

~

Reading the River

Bruce

Our ability to perceive quality in nature begins, as in art, with the pretty. It expands through successive stages of the beautiful to values as yet uncaptured by language.
—ALDO LEOPOLD, *A SAND COUNTY ALMANAC*

Back in 1995 KC and I planned to push off from the Highway D bridge headed for Imalone at the Highway A bridge. The day was cloudy and misty as we headed north on Highway 53. The radio weatherman reporting from Bloomer announced that the clouds would burn off by noon, and temperatures would reach the eighties.

We set up our cars for the D to A stretch, which our canoe guidebook informed us would be a five-hour run. We pushed off at 10:45 under a sky of fluffy dark cloud banks that looked like they disagreed with the local weather report. The river was full but not over its banks. Our guidebook told us to expect lots of rapids, a "wild and beautiful stretch."[1] When we pushed off in our red Mad River, adorned with duct tape, I announced that our goal was to make the whole trip without capsizing.

My plan to keep us upright was to focus on reading the river and applying what I knew: that the deeper channel was always on the outer bank of the bends, that dark water was deeper than the light bubbly stuff, and that when the river is wide or straight, try the middle. I also did more paddling on my knees to lower our center of gravity. My approach worked all day. The only close call was when we pushed off after lunch.

We reached the A bridge about 2 p.m., an hour and a half ahead of schedule. Deciding we had enough daylight to make it to Bruce, we repositioned our canoe and were back on the river by 2:45. The water here was wide, and the banks were sprinkled with houses. We passed our first hardwood forest of the day. The trees were spaced, leaving enough open ground to camp.

KC observed that in all our Chippewa trip so far, we had met only two other boats, and that was on Bear Lake. Many people drive by this beautiful river on their way to the boundary waters, but fewer seem to come down off the banks. They don't know what they're missing. This was the best water day we'd had. We could read the river because we actually had some river to read. KC suggested that someday we return to the Winter Dam to revisit that stretch. She also suggested we return to the West Fork after we completed the trip. We never did make it back together, so the memory of that one unusually smooth day on the river lives on undisturbed.

The sun finally broke out around four o'clock, and KC asked me, "Did you see it?" "See what?" I asked. "The patch of blue sky," she said. It made its appearance much later than the weather forecaster had predicted, but I hadn't even realized until that moment it had gotten so late in the day.

I began to notice how my time expectations had changed. When I started canoeing in my twenties, my first thought tended to be, "When will we get to the end?" By age fifty-four, I cherished every stroke of the paddle, every ripple and rapid, every new skyline of forest. If I didn't have this project, I probably wouldn't

be canoeing at all anymore. I was grateful that KC and my other
children took time to join me in the middle of their busy lives.

The Highway 8 bridge appeared at about 5 p.m., indicating
our arrival in Bruce. The day had become bright and sunny, and
we paddled through the reflection of the forest on both sides of
our red boat. I wondered out loud if the birds knew how beautiful they were. KC believed the cardinals knew—they seemed
so snooty. Eagles, she argued, weren't too self-conscious—they
just were. Speaking of eagles, we were graced during our trip by
four—or possibly one that we saw four times. Either way, it's always a sight that makes a trip that much more worthwhile. We
pulled the canoe onto the grassy left bank and called it a day.

Like all small towns along the river, Bruce began as a river and
rail center. It was established in 1884, and in 1901 it had a population of seven hundred.[2] On a rainy day in October 2012, I visited
with Richard LaBelle and Al Miller, owners of Norte Antiques in
Bruce. Richard has an appreciation for history and had gathered
some materials for me to introduce me to their hometown of
Bruce. He had just resigned his post as village president in preparation for their move to Santa Fe. Richard and Al had traveled to
Santa Fe every winter, and their desire to move there increased
with every trip. My wife, Dixie, and I met with them surrounded
by moving boxes and unboxed antiques.

I asked Richard about life in Bruce, and he described how
the railroad was taking over. The rail line wanted a clearer path
through town for the 150-car frac sand trains making their way to
the oil fields in North Dakota.

Modern-day rails bring new excitement but also controversy.
The abundance of frac sand in the Chippewa Valley has created
a surge of almost frightful demand that pits giant corporations
with deep pockets against county boards and small-town city

councils. In 2012, Canadian National Railway offered the town of Bruce twenty-five thousand dollars for permission to close one of three railroad crossings and warned the town board that if it didn't agree, the state could close the crossing anyway with no compensation. Richard, a mild-mannered but savvy retired art teacher from Cornell, told me how his negotiations with the representative from the railroad grew more tense over time: "I said, 'You were so friendly in the beginning and now you don't seem that way.'" The railroad then petitioned the state's Office of the Commissioner of Railroads to close the crossings on two roads, leaving just the Main Street crossing open. I asked Richard what he thought the state would do. "What do you think?" he asked in a cynical tone.

Norb Wurtzel and I returned to Bruce a few years later and watched a fifty-seven-car sand train pass from the porch of the MacArthur Hotel. We had returned to stay at this historic hotel and to learn more about the town. The 103-year-old MacArthur Hotel has been owned since 1987 by Donnalene David. She and her husband, Al, sold their farm to enter the hotel business. Since he passed away in 2001, the spry eighty-three-year-old manages the place. The lobby hosts the original reception desk and photos of her son, a distinguished army helicopter pilot who served in Iraq and Afghanistan.

After checking in we walked the town, passed the Bruce Theater and a number of bars. We stopped at Glory B's and then Irish Saloon. It was Wednesday night, the night of the big drawing. Soon the place was packed with people who had bought a ticket hoping for good luck. So why do people like Bruce? I asked a number of people, and all said it was peaceful. And that it was.

From our hotel porch we enjoyed the silence. Water from an afternoon rain dripped from the mill roof across the street. An occasional pickup truck passed by. An eleven- or twelve-year-old girl in a soft orange sweat suit appeared pedaling a green bike

Macarthur Hotel. RICHARD D. CORNELL

down Main Street and across the railroad tracks. As she passed us a couple of times we remarked that this is the kind of place where her parents would know she was out and safe.

The Chippewa flows beneath the Highway 8 bridge less than a mile from Norte Antiques. KC and I arrived at the bridge after paddling from the D bridge. As the river winds its way toward Bruce, it flows within sight of the Blue Hills, named for their bluish tinge. A sign at the town's edge announces Bruce as the Gateway to the Blue Hills. Among them is Flambeau Ridge. The ridge, made of extra-hard rock, resisted the movement of the glacier. Because of the strength of the rock, the Chippewa had to flow around it, creating a large curve; the area is called Big Bend.

One afternoon in July 1998, we left KC's car at Flater's restaurant, where the Flambeau River joins the Chippewa, and drove my car to the Highway 8 bridge for the next part of our journey. Our canoe guidebook predicted it would be a nine-hour trip from the bridge to Flater's, but we disregarded that advice. We had found that we could usually do the trips in half the stated time. I figured five hours. I was wrong.

This part of the river is very watery, surrounded by long stretches of marshy wetlands interspersed with hills on which some attractive houses have been built. Many of the cabins and houses were set back from the shore far enough to permit a grassy space, or as river ecologist Tom Waters would have called it, a riparian zone. My experience with the Xcel Energy dam relicensing project had educated my eye with regard to appreciating shoreline. One Wisconsin DNR study that investigated why people buy expensive waterfront property informed me that most people buy it to fish and to appreciate the beauty, but they often clear the messy-looking weeds that make good fish habitat. Thinking more about shoreline erosion, I wondered if Xcel's operation of the dams was the culprit, or if the rising and falling of floodwater wouldn't have had an equal impact. When I shared this thought with KC, she reminded me that nature doesn't cause the river to rise and fall twice a day.

KC told me she was excited about getting to the Mississippi, but strangely I was not looking forward to the end. The water was a clear brown, and we could easily see the rippled sandy bottom. Since KC has better eyesight, she was our map reader and navigator. She told me we weren't making the kind of progress we thought we would make. Concerned, we paddled on.

A marker on our map indicated an old ferry crossing, and she began to look for it intently. As we passed cabins, clusters of trailer houses, and what appeared to be a family campground, she imagined seeing the railroad bridge that would herald the spot just around every bend. We saw a large house with a couple of smaller cabins and some places that had been cleared for camping. We saw one small building with screening, which KC said was a fish-cleaning house, but no railroad bridge announcing our destination.

As the day wore on we began to be more aware of the setting sun. We retrieved our compass, watched the sun still above the tree line, and tried to figure out where we were.

An owl hooted in the woods. "That is not a good sign," KC said. "They only come out at night." Spotting a deer watching us from the bank, we stopped paddling and drifted toward it until it decided we were too close. It bounded back into the trees, probably to watch us go by. We stopped to dump the water that was sloshing around the bottom of the canoe. It felt good to stand up. I had started to get pain in my wrists from paddling.

We saw people along what looked like a boat landing on the left bank. Two pickup trucks and two couples watched the river. They asked us if we had seen any dogs. They had brought two of them down for a swim, and the animals had taken off. When we told them we hadn't seen any dogs and that we were headed for Flater's, one of them said, "Wow, that's four hours from here." Should I have asked them for a lift to Flater's? We would see.

I told KC that we would paddle until 8 p.m. before resorting to plan B—although I had no idea what plan B would be. I figured that at midsummer, we would have light until 9:30, but if we were to believe the dog owners, we were going to be in some serious trouble.

We paddled on, soon reaching Flambeau Ridge, the beginning of the famous Big Bend in the Chippewa. We were still paddling as night descended on the river, but the full moon gave us ample light. Up ahead we saw a blue light on the left bank. Our guiding star turned out to be a Pabst Blue Ribbon beer sign. We pulled in between a leisure-time pontoon boat and two ski machines, dragged our canoe onshore, and trudged toward a bar that looked like a renovated log cabin. One of the windows hosted a red Leinenkugel's neon sign. We went in.

Three couples sat at a small bar, shaking dice. We interrupted their laughter to tell them we were headed for Flater's. "Oh, that is an hour and fifteen minutes by canoe from here," one woman told us. She offered to drive us to our car. We said that it felt like the river had slowed down. "It does," a man at the bar said. "Xcel owns the river from here on down." When I mentioned this to Adam Cahow later, he confirmed that this is one of the slowest gradations on the river.

One of the women, Edi, drove KC to Flater's to pick up the car, while I had a beer and chatted with the customers at Boggie's Bar. When KC returned she told me some history she'd learned about Boggie's, which had been a gangster hangout during prohibition. Harold Flater, a local resort owner, claims that three of Al Capone's men frequented the bar and fished the river. The old house facing the river had been a brothel.

Harold Flater had worked at his resort, Flater's, for seventy-seven years when we met in 2015.[3] His son Joe had run the resort the past twenty-five years. The resort had always been in the family. Harold's dad, Harry, had sold his farm and acquired the land at the confluence of the Chippewa and Flambeau Rivers in 1938. During World War II, Harry worked at the munitions plant at Baraboo, returning to his land on weekends. He also milked cows and raised pigs to make enough to pay for the resort.

After the war, between 1946 and 1950, Harry worked on the building of the Holcombe Dam. Before the dam, Harold said, the Chippewa had a beautiful set of rapids just below his place. The rapids are below the dam pool now, but he assured me the fishing is just as good. When visitors go out to fish on the Chippewa or Flambeau, he said, "it's not unusual for them to catch over one hundred bass on their way down."

A painting by V. Remington shows the confluence of the Chippewa and Flambeau Rivers. CHIPPEWA COUNTY HISTORICAL SOCIETY

The resort's first cabin was moved down from Ladysmith, Wisconsin, and later the family added four more cabins, all built on high ground to stay dry when the river floods. The biggest flood in Harold's memory happened Labor Day weekend of 1941, when four days of heavy rain—as much as fourteen inches in some parts of Wisconsin—caused evacuations along the river. The river crested at twenty-two feet, its highest in the twentieth century.[4] But due to the family's forethought, the resort survived.

One group of visitors that still frequent Flater's includes the grandchildren of some of the first renters. "They used to come up for a week. Now all they can spare is a long weekend," Harold said wistfully.

⌒

After leaving the bar, KC and I dragged the canoe up the bank, un-loaded our stuff, and drove to pick up my car in Bruce. The owner of the bar had said we could leave the canoe there overnight. The next day, after picking up some subs for lunch, we arrived back at Boggie's at 2 p.m. and headed out. We reached Flater's in forty-five minutes, significantly less than the bar patrons had told us the night before.

Flater's sits on a short peninsula where the Flambeau River, the Chippewa's largest tributary, flows in, descending from an elevation as high as 1,570 feet above sea level.[5] It arrives at the Chippewa with an average flow of 1,750 CFS, compared to 1,500 CFS for the Chippewa at that point.[6] The river almost doubles in size when they meet. As we paddled past the Flambeau, we arrived at the headwaters of the wild Chippewa.

~

CHAPTER SEVEN

The Wild Chippewa

The Flambeau River to Jim Falls

I say there, chum, have you ever run
that stretch where the rapids roar?
And then come out with a curse and a shout,
And you're wet but you grin for more?

—THOMAS F. WATERS,
"THE CALL OF THE RIVER TRAIL"

We resumed our trip at the blue bridge below Flater's Resort, at the beginning of the legendary wild Chippewa. After visiting with Harold Flater, I knew that the placid water we would paddle through had once been beautiful rapids.

Before the dams started regulating the water flow from Holcombe to Chippewa Falls, the river fell more than two hundred feet in forty-three miles, a treacherous stretch of falls, chutes, and rapids.[1] Without knowledge of this river history you wouldn't know that the peaceful pools you see along Highway 178 between Jim Falls and Cornell conceal a legacy of wildness and death. According to local lore, ghosts still lurk in the forests along the river, crying out to be saved from the tragedy that took eleven lives below Little Falls dam in July of 1905.

Little Falls dam, 1913. WHI IMAGE ID 37820

At Farm and Fleet, I purchased an assortment of bungee cords to attach our canoes. Brian and his wife, Kari, along with Drew and KC, joined me for this trip. Brian came over on Sunday morning and helped me mount two canoes on my Honda. When Drew arrived, our small convoy headed out. Kari had never been to Cornell, and she wanted her picture next to the water tower with her last name on it. We stopped for the photo before continuing on.

At the Blue Bridge, we unloaded and were in the water by 12:15. I had estimated a three- to four-hour trip. My estimation skills had been off lately, but this didn't deter me from announcing my guess.

So there we were in the big Chippewa: KC and me in old red, Brian and Kari in their fifteen-foot Grumman, and Drew in the green solo. We had talked about the powerboats that we most likely would have to deal with, but we didn't anticipate the wind in the wide-open water. It was a gusty day, and we pushed through small whitecaps. The small gashes in the canoe that we had picked up in the rapids below Blaisdell Lake three years earlier had never given us any great problems until that day. After picking up enough water to make paddling hard work and steering difficult, we pushed into a sliver of sand shore and dumped the water. After two and a half hours of very difficult paddling, we reached Lions Club Park.

We were going to meet my wife, Dixie, at the park for a picnic, but we arrived an hour before the planned rendezvous. The kids sprawled out in the sun in front of the pavilion, while I lay on a picnic table in the shade. Having rested a while, KC and Kari went for a swim, and Brian and Drew joined me at my picnic table. When Dixie arrived, we loaded the canoes on the car and then dove into the grub she had brought. We returned to Eau Claire a very tired group in spite of the relatively easy going we had faced that day on the previously wild Chippewa.

~

The unpredictable nature of the river was a great vexation to the lumber barons. Frederick Weyerhaeuser had had enough. In 1878 he built a dam at Little Falls (present-day Holcombe), head of the wild Chippewa. The dam was 625 feet in length with thirty-two floodgates, each of which was seven feet wide and seventeen feet high.[2] On November 8, 1878, all the gates were shut to see what the dam was capable of. This caused the river in Eau Claire to fall by one foot. When the gates were opened, the released water raised the river in Eau Claire by more than four feet.[3] The flood of 1884 destroyed the dam, but not to be defeated, Weyerhaeuser hired noted dam builder Billy "the Beaver" England.[4] True to his name, the Beaver built a dam for the ages. It innovatively used the flow of the river to raise and lower the gates.[5]

The carving known as "King of the Chippewa River" now stands in a case next to the Holcombe Town Hall. CHIPPEWA COUNTY HISTORICAL SOCIETY

The city of Little Falls, at the time larger than present-day Cornell, supported this most powerful man-made structure on the river. In the mid-nineteenth century, a wood carver named Luke Lyons chiseled an eight-foot Indian that was mounted at the end of the dam. The statue, which became known as the King of the Chippewa River, was considered by lumberjacks to be their guardian spirit while they drove their logs down this difficult stretch. The Indian now stands in a glass case next to the Holcombe Town Hall.

If carved wood could talk, the former King of the Chippewa might hesitate to tell the story of the worst tragedy that occurred on its watch. On July 5, 1905, logs being sluiced through the dam got tangled in the Little Falls rapids below the dam.[6] A telegram was sent to the logging company's Chippewa Falls headquarters to request help. A crew was assembled and boarded the Omaha railroad, which ran along the eastern shore past Jim Falls and Cornell to Little Falls. Some members of the crew may have been drinking, although at least one among them, Saul Brackett of Elk Mound, was known to be a nondrinker. Saul was a student at Eau Claire High School and a star player on the 1904 state champion football team. He took the job on the driving crew—doing the dangerous work of breaking up logjams—to earn money to attend the University of Wisconsin. His father had promised him that if Saul saved five hundred dollars, he would match it.

When the crew arrived at the falls, three bateaux—flat-bottomed riverboats—were dragged from the storehouse to the shore of the raging river. An argument ensued as to how many crew members should board the first boat, which normally held ten. Foreman Andrew Gagnon ordered sixteen men onto the bateau, even though the boat was sagging under the weight. Saul beckoned one of the men, John Dressel, who could not swim: "Sit next to me, Johnny. I can swim. If we get into trouble I can help you."[7]

As the bateau reached the logjam, the men attempted to snare logs with their pike poles. Only one hooked a log, causing the boat to swing around with its rear headed downstream. The men fought to stabilize but capsized among the boulders, dumping nine crew members into the river, where they drowned. Of the seven remaining men, three, including the nonswimmer Dressel, saved themselves by jumping onto the logjam, while Saul and three others managed to cling to pieces of the boat as it headed toward the rapids. Two men were able to make it through, but Saul and the fourth man were pulled under in the current. Their bodies were recovered two days later.

Among the eleven loggers who succumbed to the rapids was Ole "Whitewater" Horne, a river legend, whose body was found near the CLB railroad bridge in Chippewa Falls. It had traveled the entire forty-mile length of the wild Chippewa over Brunet Falls, Jim Falls, Eagle Rapids, and Paint Creek Rapids. On the day of his funeral, more than one hundred loggers paid their respects, and the Norwegian businesses in Chippewa Falls closed their doors. Saul Brackett was buried near his hometown of Elk Mound, west of Eau Claire. A large gathering of fellow Eau Claire football team members and soldiers of his Wisconsin National Guard unit attended. The bank had informed Saul's father that he had achieved his five hundred dollar goal. The death of these eleven loggers was the biggest tragedy of the lumbering days on the Chippewa.

~

Following our lunch at Lions Club Park, we concluded that a lake is not a river, so we decided to skip canoeing the Holcombe Flowage and Lake Wissota. That's not to say these bodies of water aren't important to the Chippewa, however. Along with the Chippewa Flowage, they constitute the most significant residential and recreational structures in the valley, all created by Xcel Energy power plant dams.

The 2,800-acre Lake Holcombe has been a large body of water since the logging days, when the Little Falls dam created it as a huge log storage area.[8] I learned from Adam Cahow that a constant challenge of the loggers was to find a way to contain the logs in preparation for the mills. A common technique was to chain logs together into booms, barriers that were used to corral the logs floating downriver. This was such an important construct that it was part of the name of the Chippewa Lumber and Boom Company. The Little Falls dam used such a mechanism, as did the booms in Chippewa Falls, the Dells Pond in Eau Claire, and the Buffalo Slough at the Chippewa Source.

A few miles from the Holcombe Flowage, the lumber business continues into the present day. The era of floating logs downriver to sawmills ended in the early 1900s, but this didn't end logging in Wisconsin. The cutover forests were reseeded, and flourishing hardwood forests emerged. A few miles from the Holcombe Flowage off Highway 27 is the Walters Brothers lumber company. Tim Walters, the president, oversees around fifty employees, huge piles of hardwood logs, and buildings filled with humming saws.[9] They produce and sell sawed lumber, pallets, sawdust, and bark. "We sell everything but the sound," Tim said, laughing over the hum of modern-day robotics. When we entered one of the buildings, we met his son Curt as he was sharpening a saw. The saws must be sharpened every six to eight hours. Malcolm Rosholt's logging book shows pictures of men sharpening their saws in the woods. That part of logging remains, although the process has become more high-tech. The axes and saws of old times have been replaced by processors that cut a tree into twelve-foot pieces and take them to a landing, where they wait to be loaded on trucks.

Continuing our river journey, KC and I caravanned to the Holcombe Dam. Below the dam, we had to slide old red past a large recliner chair someone had deposited on the bank to create a comfortable fishing spot or maybe just to get rid of it—just one of many odd little things we'd seen along the river over the years. KC reminded me that when we started this journey, she had been too young to drive. When we passed a man and his son on Highway 29—with a canoe on their car, and the boy sleeping—she recalled similar early-morning drives when she would sleep. Much had changed in the decade-plus we had spent on this expedition.

The day was sunny, with a clear blue sky and temperatures in the seventies, and the banks were ablaze with wildflowers. As we paddled, the calm water beneath us covered the spot of the Little Falls rapids that had caused the worst tragedy of the logging era.

After a few hours of paddling, we stopped for lunch on the

swimming beach at Brunet Island State Park above Cornell. I fell out of the boat as KC pulled our canoe ashore. As I broke my fall with my right hand, a small stone lodged deep in my skin, and I had to pry it out. Ignoring the cut, I took a look around at the park where we'd landed.

Brunet Island State Park was established in 1936 when Northern States Power Company (now Xcel) donated the 168-acre island to the state. It was named after Jean Brunet, a French immigrant known as the first settler in the Chippewa Valley.[10] Today the park has twenty-four campsites with electricity and forty-five without. The Old Abe bike trail begins here and runs nineteen and a half miles to Chippewa Falls, along the former Omaha rail route. Most bike riders on the trail probably give little thought to the fact that they are riding the same route that Saul Brackett and his fellow drivers rode on the day of their death.

The 1,100-mile Ice Age Trail descends from a hill on County Road SS parallel to the west shore of the Chippewa. The trail begins at Interstate Park on the Minnesota border and ends at Potawatomi State Park near Lake Michigan. On the east shore at Cornell, the stacker rises into the sky. Located in the Mill Yard Park at Bridge Street and Park Road, it is the only known pulpwood stacker in the world. The stacker was used in Cornell from 1913 until 1972 to prepare wood for papermaking. The 175-foot remnant of the area's logging era sits alone in the city park next to the Cornell information building. The main street of Cornell is visible from the river. This is the first town we had been able to see from the river since Glidden.

At the Cornell Dam we inspected the portage, and I didn't like the looks of the rapids below the dam. On Monday, KC was to start her internship at Target, and I would be headed to Washington, DC, to teach a four-day management skills class. We decided to call it a day.

~

On July 6, 2013, Cornell celebrated its one hundredth anniversary with a large parade and celebration at the town park. A few days after attending the parade, I met with Bonnie Zinsli, its organizer, who had offered to arrange a meeting of locals to discuss Cornell history. In addition to her husband, Dick, Bonnie had invited Beverly Falbe and Lee Blanchard. Lee is the grandson of logger Louie Blanchard, whom I had read about in Walker Wyman's book *The Lumberjack Frontier*. He had been close to his grandfather, and they often fished together.

Lee inherited his grandfather's memory and interest in the past. Many of his stories and comments were validated by my previous research. I have found the knowledge and passion of people such as Lee who cherish the past to be just as valuable as the contributions of historians with advanced degrees. He told me about Bob Creek that flows into the Chippewa south of Cornell from the west. Today it flows straight into the river, but that was not always the case, Lee told me. In the logging days it curved and obstructed the logs, so the Chippewa Lumber and Boom Company straightened the creek. Lee said you can still see the outline of the old creek bed.

I much prefer hearing such details of local history like this from the mouths of those who remember them—or who have a connection to those who do. That's why I found myself returning time and again to the communities of the Chippewa River Valley, because you never know when you're going to run into someone who knows someone who knows something. On one of my trips, someone told me that Wilson Rawls, author of *Where the Red Fern Grows*, lived in Cornell for a number of years. I asked John Marder, editor of the *Courier Sentinel* at the time. As a non-native, though, he did not know whether Rawls had ever lived in the area, but he helped me put a notice in the paper that I was looking for people who knew Rawls.

Local history buff Lee Blanchard, the grandson of logger Louie Blanchard.
RICHARD D. CORNELL

The following month, I returned to Cornell for the Chippewa River Rendezvous for what would be a living portrait of life along the river in the eighteenth century, featuring American Indians, reenactors of the Eighth Wisconsin Infantry Regiment, and an Abe Lincoln impersonator. Accompanied by KC and her three boys, Logan, Stewart, and Eli, I entered the grounds to see a line of white canvas tents along the shore of the blue water of the Chippewa behind the dam. Several men dressed in Civil War uniforms displayed rifles and cooking gear, along with a large stuffed bald eagle representing the famous war eagle Old Abe, mascot of the Eighth Wisconsin Infantry. As we passed one of the tents, a woman approached me and touched my arm, asking me if I was the person who wanted to know about Wilson Rawls. She introduced herself as Virginia Ellis and told me that Rawls had been her husband's fishing and hunting partner during his time in Cornell. She had a large envelope that contained an eight-by-ten-inch photo of Woody, as he had been known locally, and a couple of articles from local papers about him.

Later on, I returned home to find an e-mail from Jane Zwiefel-hofer, whose mother, Cecilia Harms, happened to be Wilson Rawls's sister-in-law. A retired language teacher, Cecilia received me in her small, book-lined apartment at Chippewa Manor, an assisted-living facility in Chippewa Falls. When I asked her if she knew what had brought Rawls—known as Woody to those who knew him in Cornell, she replied, "Me." As she explained, Woody was looking for a place where he could hunt and fish, and his wife, Sophie, wanted to return to her hometown of Cornell to live closer to her sister.

Sophie was essential to Woody's success as a writer, as Woody himself told a reporter at the Cornell *Courier Sentinel* in one of the articles provided to me by Virginia Ellis.[11] Having grown up in a poor area of Oklahoma with little formal schooling, Woody struggled with the mechanics of writing down the stories he had in his head. He scribbled four novels and hundreds of short stories but was woefully short of confidence in his work. One day, in an explosion of frustration, he burned all of his work.

Then he met Sophie. He told her about his love of writing and that he had destroyed his work. She forced him to sit down and write as much as he could remember of his favorite story. He scribbled thirty-five thousand words, and she went to work as his editor. She wrestled the story into shape, and it became *Where the Red Fern Grows*. Rawls was reluctant to sell it, so Sophie went to work again. While it was slow to take off, the book became a huge hit among young readers, ultimately selling more than six million copies.[12] The story was made into a movie twice, in 1974 and 2003.

Woody's success took him far from Cornell, as he shared his passion for stories and writing with schoolchildren around the country. One anecdote has stuck with me because it illustrates

Wilson "Woody" Rawls came to Cornell in part because of his love of fishing.
PHOTO COURTESY OF VIRGINIA ELLIS

what his own story has meant to his readers. When he returned to Oklahoma to appear at the premiere of *Where the Red Fern Grows* in 1974, a young boy showed up and told Woody that he had walked several miles in the cold to see the film. "But," Woody said, "the film will be shown in your town next week."

"But you ain't," the boy said.

While in Cornell, Woody lived in a house on a hill that overlooked the Cornell Dam. From his front porch he could also see the grassy place that was once the log cabin of Jean Brunet, who as its first known settler is often referred to as the father of the Chippewa Valley. A historical marker on Highway 178 a short distance from Cornell marks the place of his cabin. Standing on a hill along the Chippewa, one can imagine the sound of gunfire on a New Year's Day in the mid-1800s. The Ojibwe had arrived to celebrate the New Year with Jean Brunet. They erected wigwams and warmed themselves next to the two woodstoves that heated the large cabin on the shore of the untamed river. Brunet was known as a friend of the Ojibwe. He was a friend of everyone.

During his lifetime, Brunet would have been known by the French pronunciation of his name, Bru-nay, but locals nowadays refer to him as Brunet with a hard "t" sound at the end. Brunet arrived in Chippewa Falls in 1836 and built the first sawmill on the Chippewa. After a time, he left his mill and built his cabin in Cornell, near the falls that now bear his name. He provided a service to transport boats and material around the falls, charging a fee based on weight. Studying the area of his cabin with his metal detector, Lee Blanchard told me he found a scale weight in the tall grass that he thinks might have belonged to Brunet.

Brunet's legacy was such that in 1911, William Irvine, manager of the Chippewa Lumber and Boom, motioned at a meeting to erect a monument at the Catholic Cemetery in Chippewa Falls in memory of Jean Brunet. The inscription, partially in French, reads:

> To the pious memory of the valiant pioneer Jean Brunet—
> First president of the St. John the Baptist Society of Chippewa Falls Wis. Born 1791 in Gascogne, France. Died in 1877. Builder of the first Chippewa Falls Saw Mill in 1836.[13]

Much of what is known about Brunet comes from William Bartlett's 1919 interview with Josephine Robert, the daughter of Brunet's longtime friend Francis Gauthier.[14] Josephine, who lived near Holcombe at the time, reported that Ezra Cornell visited Brunet several times while surveying the forest. It is likely Josephine was actually referring to W. J. Cornell, a distant relative of Ezra's who lived in Chippewa Falls, where he was a well-known timber cruiser, logger, and contractor. The relative was likely one

Jean Brunet, known as the first white settler in the Chippewa River Valley.
WHI IMAGE ID 37765

of Ezra Cornell's surrogates in the purchase of land in the Chippewa Valley.

Ezra himself was born in Massachusetts in 1807 and in 1829 moved to Ithaca, New York. Being quite innovative, he designed an improved plow and was a believer and supporter of telegraph technology. His investment in the Western Union Telegraph Company brought him huge wealth, which enabled him to pursue his vision of promoting learning and education. In 1857, US Representative Justin Smith Morrill from Vermont sponsored a bill that would enable sale of federal land for the building of colleges, and Ezra took advantage of the opportunity to acquire land in Wisconsin with the assistance of Henry C. Putnam, land agent in Eau Claire. Putnam was familiar with every corner and trout brook in the Chippewa Valley. In 1867, Ezra outlined plans

A memorial painting of Dylan Crabb adorns the barn at the Crabb family farm.
RICHARD D. CORNELL

for a water-power site to be located on a piece of the land scrip
surrounding Brunet Falls. He envisioned a mill at the center of
a prosperous community to be called Cornell. Following Ezra's death in 1874, the Cornell University Trustees took over the
management of his land. After letting it appreciate for several
decades, the university sold the acres for more than five million
dollars. The school had abandoned Ezra's vision for founding
a community on the valuable pine land, but residents of the
Chippewa River Valley didn't forget what he had intended. The
town that grew up around the mill was officially incorporated
as Cornell in 1913.[15]

Famous names such as Rawls and Brunet have a much wider
recognition beyond the river, but here in Cornell, the name that

Lori Crabb, pictured at Dylan's Dairy. RICHARD D. CORNELL

seems to echo in the hearts and minds of residents is that of a young local boy, Dylan Crabb, who died of cancer at age sixteen. Dylan had planned on becoming a farmer, so after he was diagnosed with leukemia in 2007, his family applied to the Make-A-Wish Foundation to fund a small dairy herd. The herd, funded by the foundation, grew as donations from community members poured in. After two failed bone marrow transplants, Dylan died on Memorial Day in 2009. Family members continued to care for the herd and then opened Dylan's Dairy, a small restaurant and ice cream parlor, in his honor.

The day I visited Dylan's Dairy with KC and her boys, I asked the older woman who was serving us if I could talk to her. The woman turned out to be Dylan's grandmother, Kari Craker, and on her break she came and sat next to me. We also met Dylan's aunt, Linda Flater, who was working that day. On a later visit to

Dylan's Dairy, I had a chat with Lori Crabb, his mother. When she talked about her son and his plans, her eyes filled with tears. Lori begins her day milking Dylan's cows with her husband. She told me that every day begins with the hole she feels over the loss, but then when she begins to milk the cows, the pain subsides. After milking, she drives into Cornell to work at a salon. Lori gave me directions to their farm and encouraged me to visit. Later at the farm, I saw the barn that features a large portrait of Dylan wearing a Wisconsin ball cap. Lingering to look at it, I found myself struck by the way the memory of this one young boy had been preserved, in ways that made sure his legacy would live on years beyond his too-brief time on earth.

We returned to the river, pushing off below the Cornell Dam. Brian and his wife, Kari, had joined KC and me for the trip to Jim Falls. The big rock ahead of us blended so well with the moving river that our first warning was a small white curl. We struggled against the current gushing from the dam. We paddled hard, but the canoe spun around, and for a few seconds we were floating backward until the boat hit the rock, and we flipped. We had experienced a glimpse of what the log drivers at Little Falls might have felt just before they fell into the rapids in 1905. My lifejacket pulled me to the top, and I wildly looked around for KC. She was struggling to hang onto the stern. Minutes before, as we scanned the rapids from shore, I had reminded Brian and Kari that canoes don't sink. "If anything happens," I said, "hang onto the boat." The river dragged me downstream, but I swam toward the canoe trying to grab the bow. When I managed to reach it, KC and I held on and floated through the rest of the rapids with our canoe between us. These rapids must have been the remnants of rapids below Brunet Falls. If we had had the presence of mind to look toward the west shore, we would have seen the place where Jean Brunet's cabin once stood.

KC and me floating in the river with the canoe after it flipped in the rapids.
BRIAN CORNELL

Brian and Kari made it through on the left and floated toward us with the intent to help. I warned them to stay away; too many people have drowned in these situations trying to help others. We floated for a quarter of a mile until I was able to grab a branch of a dead tree and pull us to shore. We flipped the canoe to get rid of the water and were back on our way. I lost my sunglasses and river hat that I wore every day of our trip, but was grateful for not losing more. I had feared these rapids from the first time I saw them as we arrived at the dam, but I had tensed up and forgotten to pay attention. In the end, all was well and Brian took a picture of KC and me in our green lifejackets hanging onto the red canoe and smiling. I have it pinned to the corkboard in my writing room. We paddled for the rest of the day in calm waters, but I couldn't shake the fear I had felt since before we set out for the day. I always fear and respect the river. Maybe that is what drew me to it.

Just above the Jim Falls dam, we pulled up on a boat ramp on the west side of the river. We had popped some screws from the bow of old red—a real river warrior now. I began to grumble about the dams to KC. "Fine, you skip 'em," KC said, "and I'll go back with the solo and do the parts we missed." She won me over, and we continued on together. In fact, I'd like to return to the landing and paddle to Jim Falls someday. The dams are a part of the river now.

Standing next to the Old Abe marker along Highway 178 on a Sunday evening, I could hear the roar of high-powered racing engines from behind the tall pines across the road. The marker is located on the land once owned by Dan McCann, who bought Old Abe from Chief Sky. The source of the engine roar was Eagle Valley Raceway. I first visited the raceway on a Saturday afternoon, hoping I could meet the owner. I parked in front of the Old Barn Tavern on a hill overlooking the track and noticed a man in his forties was leaving. I don't know why but I thought he might be the owner and asked him if it was his place. When it turned out I was right, I introduced myself, gave him my card, and told him my mission. "I don't have time to talk with you now," said the man, Jerry Weigal. "Everything is going wrong." He wasn't sure if the track was ready for the next day's race but had been working on it. I asked him how he got it ready. He said he dragged it and drove around with his tractor.

The track is a three-eighths-mile clay oval. Jerry had owned the place for fourteen years. When I returned on Sunday to observe the proceedings, Jerry and another man were working on the track with a couple of trackers, as other employees began to arrive. Three women entered the food stand and began preparations. A couple of men opened the ticket stand. I overheard one guy ask if he would be able to drive the tow truck. Then the race cars began to arrive. Some were towed behind pickups, some in their own covered van. They arrived on a side road and entered a parking space. This was the pit. A man in a bright green vest climbed the flagman podium and unwound his flags: white, orange, green, and checkered. The enthusiastic voice of a local radio celebrity welcomed us. He announced the sponsors for the race and that a woman on one of the morning spots was here.

A white Silverado pickup with a tank on the back circled the track spraying water onto the surface. A deep-throated roar echoed from the pit as the race cars started waking up. Four cars followed each other from the entry and zipped around the track. After a few spins, the flagman gave the green, and they moved into race mode, sliding around the turns and barreling through the stretches. After a few laps, the flagman threw down white, then checkered. The cars exited through a back drive, and the Silverado appeared to sprinkle the track again. Four more cars arrived and repeated the warm-up scenario. Finally, all was ready for the first heat. "These guys know what they are doing," I thought to myself. Then I saw the red EMS vehicle parked at the edge of the pit. There was danger here, and I wondered if the risk was part of what attracted the drivers. I couldn't stay for the whole show. I drove down the long road past the Old Abe memorial, thinking about risk and danger and the reasons we undertake certain challenges. I was headed for Jim Falls, the place where Old Abe's story takes flight.

⁓

CHAPTER EIGHT

Shaping a River

Jim Falls to Lake Wissota

Men may dam it and say they have made a lake, but it will still be a river. It will keep its nature and bide its time.
—WENDELL BERRY, *THE UNFORESEEN WILDERNESS*

On the day we returned to Jim Falls, the sky was rolling with gray clouds, and a mild wind stirred the air around the river. I was concerned about paddling in the wide pools behind the dams, not so much because of any danger but because of the discomfort.

After breakfast in Chippewa Falls, KC followed me up Highway 178 to Jim Falls. She parked and got in my car with me for some scouting, but we couldn't see a portage around the Jim Falls dam. We met a couple of men who worked for Xcel Energy working on a substation above the dam. While they weren't much help in our search for the portage, they filled us in on what happens at a substation.

The substation was located below a sloping hill that crested above the river. The deep and spongy grass gave us a little bounce as we walked. We learned that before the new dam this was a canal, or spillway, for surplus water to get around the old dam. Another channel is visible from a closed iron bridge over the river.

Since the building of the dam, it is a channel of dry rocks: a slice of the riverbed of the once wild Chippewa.

The Xcel Energy employees offered us a tour of the power plant. After one of them made a call, a pickup truck from the power company arrived a few minutes later. The driver, Mike, resembled a classic Old West lawman, tall and thin with a white mustache. Give him a six-shooter on his hip, and he would have fit on the dusty streets of Dodge. He would be our tour guide.

Inside the plant, we heard the hum of the three generators that spun like inverted tops. They were neatly secured to the clean cement floor. Our guides told us about a giant circuit breaker that would prevent the system from being blown out if a line went down. Impressive gauges and instruments lined a wall, and Mike explained what they were while we pretended to understand. One was called an exciter, which opened all the gates. Another was a moving drum with a pen that traced the depth of the river, which could vary by up to two feet on rare occasions. We followed Mike down a set of tightly curled steps to see where the action was. Below, a giant turbine turned as water fell on it and spun a shiny metal cylinder. Electricity generated by the mechanism surged out of a copper wire somewhere above us and below the dam; the falling water made its contribution and returned to its channel on its way to the Mississippi.

Mike showed us pictures of the great flood of 1941 that wiped out what was then known as the new dam. At the edge, we saw the water boiling out as it left the powerhouse. This is what danger looks like, Mike said. We thanked him, and he gave us a booklet on the dams as we parted ways.

A large reservoir pools behind Jim Falls, one of the largest energy producers in the Midwest. Before the dam, the river had quite a different look. This is how Father Charles Goldsmith described the area of the untamed Chippewa when he came up from Chippewa Falls to dedicate St. Ann's Church on November 15, 1886:

Traveling up the Chippewa from here one crosses the mouths of the Yellow River, Paint Creek and a number of smaller streams. A picturesque rapids or falls beginning at a place which is called after the first justice of the peace appointed for this region by Governor Doty, "Jim Ermatinger's" (or Jim's); the river forcing its way between high banks covered with pine, cedar and hemlock, dashes over a rocky bed in a succession of cascades which have their beginning at Brunet's Falls, eighteen miles above.[1]

We looked for the boat landing that Mike said was below the dam and resumed our trip. Spotting a couple of houses for sale, we talked about getting our own place along the Chippewa someday: the Cornell Lodge, a family place we would all own and pass on. Why not dream a little? You never know.

Chippewa Falls and Eau Claire might seem to dominate the river scene because of their size, but the smaller river communities— Glidden, Winter, Cornell, Bruce, and Jim Falls—make up the heart of the Chippewa River Valley. There is nothing small about life in these places. I visited Jim Falls on a number of occasions. While portaging around the Jim Falls dam on one of these visits, KC and I drove through the downtown and saw only empty stores and a couple of bars. I never stopped that day, but later learned that appearances can be deceiving. On a later visit, we saw markers explaining the significance of the very large sculpture of Old Abe overlooking the Chippewa. A couple of other markers announced that the Xcel power plant and the local cheese factories were the largest in Wisconsin. Every town on the Chippewa has its stories, including this one.

Over the years I had read about the local Sturgeon Festival at Jim Falls and returned to check it out, arriving at the falls via

Highway S, which connects Highways 27 and 178. Along the way I passed the grounds of Country Fest, which in 1987 became the first large summer music festival in the valley. The first festival featured Tanya Tucker and the Nitty Gritty Dirt Band. Seven years later festival organizers launched Shake, Rattle, and Roll, later changed to Rock Fest. That festival featured the Guess Who, Cheap Trick, and REO Speedwagon.[2]

When I arrived for the Sturgeon Festival on August 31, 2014, I wondered if I could find some people fishing for the event's namesake. I tried asking a woman at the local gas station if anyone was fishing for sturgeon, but she didn't know. My curiosity would have to go unsatisfied for another few hours.

As I drove through town I noticed a number of empty chairs lined the street. At Randy's Jim Town Inn, the women behind the bar told me that the center of action was the Lions Club about a mile away. As I headed in that direction, I spotted a small group of people downhill to my left. It was the parade staging area.

Finally I arrived at Anson Park. This is the place Doug Faulkner, geography professor at University of Wisconsin–Eau Claire, believes to be the start of the Lower Chippewa.[3] A large number of people were setting up craft displays. I parked and headed for the Lions Club building across the road, where a man was handing out orange vests to three guys. He turned out to be Bob Rosenburg, chair of the Sturgeon Festival, which seemed to make him the right person to ask about sturgeon fishing. I found out that the fishing wouldn't begin until the following day, per DNR rules. He told me more about the park, which the community had acquired just a few years back with a big donation from a local bar owner. The Lions have developed it, including the addition of stairs down to the river. Rosenburg then suggested that I talk to his co-chair, Larry Bradley, who was making brats. According to Larry, this was the forty-fifth year that the Lions had sponsored the event. He showed me the way to the stairs, where a lone fisherman was set up at the bottom. Leaving him in peace, I returned to the park in time to hear the sound of a hymn floating up from the pavilion. It was the choir from the local Methodist Church.

I strolled back to my car past a number of vendors: an artist carving wood with a chain saw, a display for Absolute Power Sports, a quilt maker, and a purveyor of plaques. Back at the parking lot, I chatted with one of the festival volunteers in orange vests. Elmer Wold identified himself as a member of Chippewa Falls Moose Club No. 246. I asked him about his experiences at the festival, and he shared one memorable story. A few years earlier, he said, he had brought his eighty-year-old sister from Durand to the festival. Some motorcyclists arrived and parked. His sister said she had never been on a motorcycle, so he asked one of the bikers if he would take her, and the rider obliged. They took a picture of her on the bike and used it on her Christmas card that year. To this day she regrets she never got the name of that biker. "Maybe he will read your book and come back," Elmer said.

My return route took me back through the town, which I now saw was a couple of miles long. More empty chairs had arrived in front of the houses. One man was already sitting along the road waiting for the parade, set to begin in another hour and a half. For me the rows of empty chairs signified hope: the gatherings of people who keep these town events alive, and their dedication to the small things that make life here interesting.

One time when KC and I were at Jim Falls, we drove over the bridge and up 178 to Old Abe Park, where a bronze plaque gives the history of Old Abe, the mascot of the Wisconsin Eighth. I first encountered the story of Old Abe at Park Falls, where a large statue has been erected in the bird's honor. KC told me she had read in a children's book that an Indian had sold the eagle to a farmer who lived near Bob's Creek. While researching Jean

The Old Abe statue in Jim Falls. RICHARD D. CORNELL

Brunet's story, I came across a more complete account of the famed bird by historian Richard Zeitlin.

According to Zeitlin, Old Abe began life in his nest in a tall pine near the headwaters of the Flambeau River.[4] When Ojibwe Chief Sky (Ahgamahwegezhig) killed the mother eagle, he rescued the eaglet and sold it for one bushel of corn to Dan and Margaret McCann, who lived across the river from Jim Falls. Lee Blanchard, a local history buff I met in Cornell, questioned the bushel of corn part of the story, based on details of the story he had picked up along the way. "My guess is that the corn in question more likely was in a jar or two," Lee had told me.

Lee is the grandson of logger Louie Blanchard, whom I had read about in Walker Wyman's book *The Lumberjack Frontier*. He had been close to his grandfather, and they shared a love of fishing and an interest in the past. Many of his stories and comments were validated by my previous research. I have found the knowledge and passion of people such as Lee who cherish the past to be

The Eighth Wisconsin Infantry Regiment poses with Old Abe in 1863.
WHI IMAGE ID 1945

just as valuable as the contributions of historians with advanced degrees. Sure enough, buried in Zeitlin's notes is a suggestion that the expression "bushel of corn" was really a euphemism for liquor.

On the receiving end of the exchange was Dan McCann, a talented musician. Old Abe hopped and fluttered his wings when Dan played "Bonaparte's Retreat" on his fiddle. Impressed by the eagle's seeming patriotism and unable to fight in the war himself due to a disability, McCann offered the eagle to the Chippewa Falls militia. When they declined McCann's offer, Captain John E. Perkins of the Eau Claire Badgers purchased him for $2.50 for the Eau Claire group, which became Company C of the Eighth Regiment. In September of 1861 the group, by this time called the Eagles in honor of their mascot, marched into Camp Randall in Madison to the tune of "Yankee Doodle." Old Abe grasped the company flag and flapped and stretched his wings. A Madison newspaper described the event as a majestic sight.

At the battle of Corinth on October 3, 1862, Old Abe took off when bullets severed his leash. As eagle bearer—which had become an unofficial honorary position in the unit—David Mc-Clain chased after him as the bird flew down the federal line. Confederate bullets riddled McClain's shirt and trousers. McClain caught the eagle, held him under his shirt, and ran for cover. Mc-Clain risked life and limb because the bird had become such an important morale booster for the Union soldiers, in the Wisconsin Eighth and beyond. At the same time, he had become such a thorn to the Confederacy that Confederate General Sterling Price offered a reward for Old Abe's head. He wasn't successful and Old Abe appeared in more than two dozen battles. In the duration of the war, the Wisconsin Eighth and its revered mascot traveled about fifteen thousand miles in seven states by foot, rail, and ship.

After the war Old Abe retired to claim his celebrity. He traveled from his new home in Madison to appear in parades and at veterans' rallies. He died on March 26, 1881. Today a likeness of Old Abe appears on the left shoulder patch of the US Army's 101st Airborne Division—an elite unit known as the Screaming Eagles. In Wisconsin, imagery of Old Abe can be found up and down the Chippewa Valley and beyond. At Memorial High School in Eau Claire, which has adopted the eagle as its mascot, a statue of Old Abe stands proudly overlooking the school.

～

On July 13, 2000, KC and I caravanned to Chippewa Falls, turning onto Highway J so we could see what was happening at the Chippewa Dam. Awaiting us was an awesome sight. At least two gates were open, and the powerhouse must have been running at full steam—or rather, full turbine. The river was foaming and fast all the way to the bridge below.

Water gushes through the gates at Chippewa Dam. RICHARD D. CORNELL

KC parked her car near the bridge at O'Neil Creek. We walked over the pedestrian bridge and studied the area looking for landmarks for when we would arrive back at this spot by boat. We read a sign describing the former Chippewa Village. All that remained was a collection of five dilapidated buildings that once served collectively as a motel. At one time, this had been a thriving area of commerce and home to a trading post owned by Michel Cadotte. A sign informed us that in the 1800s, Chippewa Village had two hundred residents. Marge Hebbring, a descendant of Cadotte and a docent at the Chippewa County Historical Society, noted that Cadotte was considered an extremely valued and important trader by the Ojibwe. She also said that the Stanley brothers' first sawmill had been located here. Apparently the Chippewa had a number of "first" sawmills. We headed for Jim Falls.

We crossed the Highway 178 bridge into Jim Falls. Looking at the dam, we saw all the gates were closed—a good sign. After driving up and down the road that runs through Jim Falls, we finally found the boat landing and pushed off in the red canoe. Staying along the west shore, we just missed hitting a dock. A couple of dogs saw us and raced along the bank. At this point we were paddling through an area of geological significance. Jim Falls stands at the beginning of the Wissota terrace, which can be traced the length of the valley. The terrace was created by sediment deposited by glacial outwash.

The wind picked up, coming up the river diagonally across our bow from the left, and the channel was filled with whitecaps. I began to worry about how we would get past this difficult stretch of river. I knew the river was wider downstream.

We had paddled less than an hour when we came to a small beach, a patch of sand about five feet wide and twenty yards long. We knew from experience that such places were rare, so we agreed to stop for lunch. KC immediately began studying the shore, collecting rocks she could use in school projects. "I'm always a teacher," she said with a laugh. She saw some small animal bones, which we gathered up in one of our bags. I laid back and watched the clouds as KC continued her explorations. When I arose some time later, she was downriver, out of sight. For one second, I was worried, but as I got up, I could see the top of her blond hair in the tall grass. I lay back down and continued my cloud watching. When she was satisfied that her exploration was complete, she bounced back and perched next to me. We talked about the time below the Winter Dam, when I was fly-fishing and Brian had been along, and we played on a sandbar for a while.

We had experienced few opportunities for simple reflection during these trips, always having a goal to achieve, a journey to complete. I studied the water and felt the wind as it came gusting up the channel. Then it seemed to calm, and the water had fewer

The wild Chippewa, downriver of the Chippewa Dam on a day when the gates were open. RICHARD D. CORNELL

whitecaps. This was one of the first times when I actually studied the river and contemplated the wind. KC wondered where the wind came from. I almost said something about the movement of the earth and high and low pressure systems, but it didn't seem like the right time to get too scientific. "Good question," I said instead.

I noticed we were at one of the narrowest places thus far, but we could see the channel widen out downriver, and I knew we would have an easier time of it along the west shore. We watched the water calm and stir up again, waiting for our best chance to cross. Since there didn't seem to be a right time to start, we just started.

I steered us diagonally, doing my best to keep us pointed into the waves. We didn't talk; we knew we had an important project. We dug in hard and studied those waves as if our lives depended on it. We weren't in danger, but if we flipped it would be a real mess to get ourselves upright again. We reached the other side together and saw some scattered patches of green plants all waving about four feet above the water line. KC thought it might be wild rice and that it would be fun to harvest some. We approached the grass and I paddled her into them. She giggled as the waving grass brushed her hand. "This is more fun than the river," she said, laughing. We studied our weeds. The stalks were hollow and had seeds, so we decided it wasn't wild rice. She broke off a couple with some difficulty, and they ended up taped in my journal.

Now close to the west shore, safe from the wind that continued to whip up the middle, we paddled along and appreciated the flowers. Shortly we heard laughter and saw several adults sitting on a deck outside a small cabin, boats docked in a line, and a group of boys wrestling in the water and three more on the deck. We were at Mallard's Resort.

Downstream from the resort, sandstone formations began to appear on the riverbank. We studied the structures and the blue and pink wildflowers hanging from them until arriving at a place where a small creek entered. We followed it upstream to a quiet pool surrounded on both sides by high hills and more rock formations. A small cave at the end had probably been created by the erosion of big floods over the years. As the light dimmed, the sounds of the river gave way to the silence of the cove. We stroked the water lightly and glided, embracing the moment.

We returned to the Chippewa and paddled on. As we approached Lake Wissota, the river widened, the number of boats increased, and the rock formations continued. Ahead on the right we could see the biggest rock structure we'd seen. We figured that O'Neil Creek, our stopping point for the day, would be just on the other side.

After we paddled around the end of the dells and into a backwater-like pool, the walk bridge came into view. We paddled up the O'Neil Creek to the parking lot. As we were pulling our canoe ashore, KC called out, "Dad, look at that!" and pointed to a wild rose growing on the steep embankment. She stashed the flower in our cooler, and we finished strapping our canoe onto the car. We were at the head of Lake Wissota.

Lake Wissota is a 6,024-acre lake that lies behind the dam that creates it. Named after Wisconsin and Minnesota, it conceals the Yellow River, Paint Creek, O'Neil Creek, and Eagle Rapids. At the edge of the lake is Lake Wissota State Park. Opened in 1972, the park covers 1,062 acres and has eighty-one campsites.[5]

I joined Tony Schuster, an avid outdoorsman and world traveler as well as a dedicated volunteer on the Ice Age Trail, at his home overlooking the lake a short distance from the dam.[6] Before he retired as vice president of NSP, his job for many years was to manage the flow of the river by overseeing the dam operators who were responsible for making decisions in high water, low water, and ice. As we looked out over Wissota, I referred to it as a lake, but Tony called it a reservoir. I asked him about the environmental consequences of the dam, including the effects of water temperature on the ecosystem. "The water on top is certainly warmer than that of a free-flowing river, [but] there is no doubt in my mind of the value of the dams which produce renewable non-polluting energy," he said with confidence.

Rob Olson, who manages the power plants on the river, shares Tony's respect for the operators. "They need the skill of an engineer and a hydrologist," Olson said. "When I skate or bike along the river, I imagine that those molecules came from Park Falls."[7]

CHAPTER NINE

Turning Points

Chippewa Falls

*In valleys, everything runs downhill, and all kinds of ter-
restrially derived organic matter moves down valley slopes
to stream channels providing energy and nutrients to the
stream's inhabitants.*

—THOMAS F. WATERS, *WILDSTREAM*

The map says Chippewa Falls, but people in the area simply call it
Chippewa. In the very early days it was known as "the falls." It is
the only town on the Chippewa that carries the name of the river.

Chippewa Falls is a place of transition. It is here where the
pine forest fades and the hardwoods begin. And below this spot,
the river channel gradually begins to change from bedrock to
gravel. The Ojibwe had a significant presence here. Michel Cadotte had his trading post on the falls in the 1800s, and Father
Charles Goldsmith started one of the first churches at the falls.
In Chippewa Falls, I encountered three people—Chuck Card,
Marge Hebbring, and Dick Leinenkugel—who represented the
intersection of history and heritage that happened here. Chuck's
great-grandfather and grandfather worked in the Big Mill, a large
lumber mill on the Chippewa River owned by the Chippewa

A postcard shows Chippewa Falls before the dam was built.
CHIPPEWA COUNTY HISTORICAL SOCIETY

Lumber and Boom Company, while Marge, a volunteer at the Chippewa County Historical Society, can trace her Ojibwe heritage to Michel Cadotte. Dick is the third-generation custodian of the iconic Leinenkugel's brewery.

It's Christmas in Chippewa Falls. At Irvine Park headlights are turned off, and cars slowly line up to enter the Christmas Village. They pass under a lighted arch and into a jeweled world of liquid color made up of more than seventy thousand lights. A 1900s cardboard football team dressed in brown crouch, ready to charge. Children in the cars press their noses against the windows to drink it all in. The awesome display is a community project made up of hundreds of people who work in teams to see their visions become reality, not unlike the community itself.

Visitors arriving at the park coming in from the south would have passed over the dark river within sight of the NSP dam and up Bridge Street. They also would have passed the Mason Shoe Outlet Store, representing one of the largest distributors of shoes

William Irvine, manager of Chippewa Lumber and Boom.
CHIPPEWA COUNTY HISTORICAL SOCIETY

in the United States, and Leinenkugel's brewery, both historical icons of the logging days. The park is named for William Irvine, who donated 318 acres of land to the city to build it in 1906. Irvine wanted to establish the park to protect this scenic slice of the Chippewa Valley from development and preserve its beauty for everyone's enjoyment. He set aside a trust for upkeep of the park, with the requirement that the land never be used to sell goods for profit. The land also includes a preserved schoolhouse, log cabin, zoo and petting zoo, and the Glen Loch Dam.[1]

Irvine's legacy to Chippewa Falls began in 1855 when Frederick Weyerhaeuser of the Chippewa Lumber and Boom Company hired him to manage the Big Mill, at the time the largest mill in the world under one roof. Rebuilt in 1887 after a fire, the mill had

Chuck Card, whose grandfather and great-grandfather worked in the Big Mill, at his eightieth birthday party. RICHARD D. CORNELL

peak daily production of 336,354 board feet—a measurement of twelve-by-twelve-by-one-inch blocks of lumber—in 1905.[2]

Chuck Card's great-grandfather Otis and grandfather Charles worked in the mill.[3] When Weyerhaeuser and Irvine closed the mill, they gave the cutover land they owned to the employees, including Chuck's grandfather Charles. Chuck has a copy of a land deed signed by Irvine and Weyerhaeuser, which he stores in a safe. Today the water of Lake Wissota covers that land, and Chuck has a home overlooking the lake. He loves to canoe and cherishes the wild areas.

On April 24, 2016, the community threw a party for Chuck's eightieth birthday, and I drove over from St. Paul to learn why Chuck had become such a popular figure in town. More than two hundred people gathered, greeted the guest of honor, partook of the ten yards of dessert, sat around tables, and visited. A two-man band with a trumpet and guitar played on the stage. I asked several of the attendees how Chuck managed to acquire so many friends, and found out that he is literally Santa Claus. "He has played Santa for the town kids for as long as I can remember," one old-timer told me. Card's daughter had tears in her eyes when I asked her. "He does anything people ask of him," she answered. So it goes beyond the actual physical resemblance, from his beard to his kind eyes; he has a reputation for generosity. I became convinced that if you asked him for a gift, he would probably give it to you. According to his son, he also shares my passion for canoeing, mostly up in the Boundary Waters of Minnesota, but also along the Chippewa.

While celebrating Chuck, I had the chance to wander around the building and became intrigued with its history as well. The party was held at the Heyde Center for the Arts, formerly McDonell Memorial High School. The former school was built in 1907 by lumberman Alexander McDonell, who gifted it to Notre Dame Parish in memory of his wife. In 1983 the large brick building was placed on the National Register of Historic Places. From the upper steps leading into the building, you can look down and see patches of the Chippewa River pool behind the NSP dam. You can also see most of downtown, including the former headquarters of the Chippewa Lumber and Boom.

From the building portico you can look to your left and see the Church of Notre Dame. Father Charles Goldsmith built the church in 1870. A convent was added in 1884, four years after Goldsmith's death. Today the convent building houses the Chippewa County Historical Society and Genealogy Society, which is staffed by a small group of passionate volunteers, including Chuck. The museum has rooms dedicated to the logging era, a typical school from those days, a nun's bedroom, and Ojibwe history. A passageway leads from the museum down to the

Goldsmith Memorial Chapel where Father Goldsmith is buried beneath the altar.

Father Goldsmith arrived in Chippewa Falls in 1869, after being ordained at the American College in Louvain, Belgium, in 1868. He traveled to the La Crosse Diocese, where he was assigned to Chippewa Falls. The growing city presented a challenging assignment, as J. A. Anderson, Goldsmith's biographer, described: "It was not an inspiring story nor an inviting picture. . . . There were various nationalities and varied natures all requiring different treatment for their various spiritual and mental ailments."[4] He boarded a steamboat on May 25, 1896, and headed up the Mississippi. At Wabasha he boarded the *Monitor* for the trip up the Chippewa to Eau Claire. From there he traveled by land to the falls.

After celebrating his first mass at St. Mary's of the Falls on May 27, 1869, he began to raise funds to build a new church. While canvassing the logging camps of the Chippewa for financial support, he met more than 800 men, 440 of whom contributed a total of $2,300 for the church, to be called Notre Dame. Anderson wrote that this "warmed his heart forever afterward for 'his boys.' . . . and never to his last day did he lose interest in the pinery boys of the Chippewa."[5]

Father Goldsmith worked every day to advance his parish. He led in expanding and developing the schools that stood on Catholic Hill and "command[ed] a view of the winding little stream [Duncan Creek] at their feet, of the sweeping Chippewa which rolls on under the glistening sun-light, of the pretty little city."[6] He spoke on the importance of developing a taste for literature and encouraged the creation of a reading circle.

Until 1877, Father Goldsmith had been the sole leader of the parish. On April 8 of that year he called a meeting of the men of the parish to form the first church committee. One of its members was Jacob Leinenkugel. His concern for the sick led Father Goldsmith, with the help of the ladies of the Aid Society, to create the first hospital in a small home on the hill. The hospital ran out of space quickly, and the Hospital Sisters of St. Francis purchased the larger Rutledge property on Pearl Street in September of 1885. Managed by Sister Rosa, it stood without peer in northern Wisconsin at the time.[7]

In 1887 Father Goldsmith's health began to fail, but he carried on serving his parish, which had grown to 534 families and 2,800 communicants by 1888. It was the largest parish in the state outside of Milwaukee.[8] Father Goldsmith's last public appearance was on July 11, 1890, at a meeting of the Ancient Order of Hibernians. "He was driven home, leaving a hall filled with gay and happy banquetters, and there alone on the hill amid his well-loved pines he gave way to a hemorrhage more severe and prostrating than any before endured."[9] He died on November 24, 1890.[10]

Marge Hebbring knows Chuck as a fellow volunteer for the local history museum, where they have worked alongside each other to share and celebrate old photographs, Native foods, and a homemade birchbark canoe. The museum has even organized demonstrations of axe throwing, a pastime enjoyed by lumberjacks during colonial times.

While Chuck is closely connected to the lumber history of the area, Marge could fill me in on the history of its French-Ojibwe fur trade. It is believed that a large Ojibwe village once stood on the hill where the Notre Dame complex is located now. Another old village was located at the confluence of Duncan Creek and the Chippewa near Chippewa Falls. These villages became important trading posts during the fur-trading era. "Traders set up their operations wherever there were rapids because this was the place people coming up- and downriver had to stop to portage their canoes," Marge explained to me.[11] The Chippewa splashed over Belille Falls (near present-day Radisson), Little Falls (Holcombe), Brunet Falls (Cornell), Jim Falls, and Chippewa Falls.

Marge Hebbring, a descendent of famed Chippewa Valley trader Michel Cadotte, is
pictured at the Chippewa County Historical Society, where she volunteers.
RICHARD D. CORNELL

Chippewa Falls was particularly significant as the last place a
steamboat could reach by making its way upriver from the Mississippi, and then only when the water was high.

Thanks to Donna Bourget at the museum, I was able to see
photographs of all of the falls that had once been trading posts.
Donna sits in a little room with a computer, printer, scanner, and
a treasure of old photographs and postcards. She grew up in the
village of Cadott along the Yellow River, a Chippewa tributary
that flows past the town and into Lake Wissota. A park near the
river features a memorial to Michel Cadotte, with a wood carving under glass representing the trader. Nearby a drawing shows
the geology of the area. Donna's father once owned the feed mill
along the Yellow River. He liked to take photographs and collected hundreds of slides, which Donna used to create a pictorial

A painting by an unknown artist shows the first sawmill on the Chippewa, built by Jean Brunet at Chippewa Falls. WHI IMAGE ID 4710

slide show entitled *Cadott—Then and Now*. It is a thoughtful study of the rise and fall of a small town.[12]

On our downriver trip, KC and I arrived at Allen Park and watched Duncan Creek flow toward the Chippewa. And a special place this is. Imagine the fadeout images in that area: Indian camps in the 1700s, the first sawmill built in 1836 by Jean Brunet. Brunet's mill was later replaced by the Big Mill, until the sawmills gave way to new industries. Eventually, those too became relics of the past, leaving shells and empty buildings at the center of Chippewa Falls. In 1999 the city took steps to revitalize its downtown area, which included plans for a riverfront park to capitalize on what remained its main asset, the Chippewa River.[13]

When we visited, the Chippewa was high, water gushing through one gate of the dam. After scouting the area we decided the best entry point was Duncan Creek and found a nice, well-used path partially hidden by tall grass. We unloaded old red from our car and packed her up at the edge of the creek, where the water was almost waist high. We felt that if we got through the first ten minutes without flipping we'd have it made for the day. We paddled down the short stretch of the creek into the Chippewa, hugging the calmer water of the right bank at the edge of the heavy flow from the powerhouse. We'd been out less than five minutes when a huge something rolled in the water to our right. It had a brown yellowish body and could have been a sturgeon. Whatever it was, we realized it could have capsized us if it had brushed our canoe.

We paddled on. Water gushed from a pipe to our right, and we wondered if it came from the Amoco Foam Products plant. Parallel with Highway 29 we could smell the diesel exhaust. We heard a train whistle. We passed under the first bridge downriver from the power plant and reached the Highway 53 bridge. Above us on the high bank was the former home of the genius who brought, following the Big Mill, the second big thing to Chippewa Falls. It was the home of Seymour Cray Jr., who designed and built the world's fastest computer along the banks of the Chippewa.

Cray loved the river. He played in it as a child, and after a successful career working on early computing technologies, he returned to the Chippewa to follow his ultimate dream. He wanted to design and build the world's biggest and fastest computer—a supercomputer. He began at a small lab in Hallie, a village roughly halfway between Chippewa Falls and Eau Claire. His dream would result in creating a company of close to five thousand employees.[14] The economic impact still resonates up and down the valley, leading him to become one of the most celebrated figures along the Chippewa.

Cray's father arrived in Chippewa Falls in 1925 to work at NSP. With a degree in civil engineering from the University of Minnesota, he was hired to help build the dam and power plant that still stand today. During his first few months, he and his wife lived in a tent. When the dam was finished he joined the city as its first city engineer. He stayed at his post for thirty-eight years. Rod Pike, Clay's successor, occupied the position for another thirty-eight years. When Rod took over, he found the elder Seymour's University of Minnesota transcript in his desk: all A's. He gave it to Seymour Junior's son Stephen, who is a judge in Chippewa County. In a phone call, Rod gave me some insight into the less-famous Seymour of the family. "Seymour Senior worked during the Depression and was able to accomplish a great deal with few resources," Rod told me. "He had to borrow surveying equipment from NSP, and he managed the construction of the City Hall." Rod was a part of the team that named a highway into the city as Seymour Cray Sr. Blvd.[15]

After returning to the valley, Seymour Junior established his first lab at the town of Hallie south of Chippewa Falls. Hallie is an incorporated community located along Lake Hallie, an oxbow lake that was once a part of the Chippewa River. In 1976 Cray Research sold its first supercomputer to Los Alamos National Laboratory.[16]

After the founders of Cray Research sold the first few machines, believing that the worldwide market would top out at fifty computers, the business exploded and expanded into Chippewa Falls. The company constructed a series of buildings along the river across from the town. Rod Pike remembers that time as exciting but challenging for the city: "The company was moving so fast, we could barely keep up building water and sewer connections for the expansion."[17] The ten-million- to twenty-million-dollar computers were loaded onto trucks. Tucked in with each computer was a case of Leinenkugel beer.[18]

⌒

In its heyday, Cray occupied a number of buildings on the south side of the river. Employees driving into work would turn off before the big bridge leading into town. A long curve took them to Park Street. They would have passed the small, eight-sided, white building on the south side of the road. This is the home of one of the most famous places in town: Chippewa Springs, source of what locals believe to be the purest water in the world. Its first owner was Ezra Pound's grandfather.

Thaddeus Pound settled in Chippewa Falls in 1856. He served as speaker of the Wisconsin Assembly, lieutenant governor, three-term US Congressman, and president of the Union Lumber Company. In 1889 he established the Chippewa Springs Health Club and began bottling Chippewa Spring Water. About this time he built the springhouse that still stands along Park Street across from the present-day bottling company. Also around this time his son Homer moved to Hailey, Idaho. This is where Thaddeus's grandson Ezra—author of more than seventy books and one of the most influential voices in poetry and literature—was born. When Ezra was still young, Homer left Idaho for Philadelphia and later Europe.

While Ezra never lived along the Chippewa, he must have felt some affinity to the home of his grandfather. When Thaddeus Pound contributed writings to the book *Chippewa County, Wisconsin: Past and Present,* Ezra submitted a poem in the style of Henry Wadsworth Longfellow's "Song of Hiawatha."[19] The poem, "Legend of the Chippewa Spring and Minnehaha, the Indian Maiden," references the famed spring of Chippewa Falls:

> Thus it was that Hiawatha,
> On the Chippewa's southern slope,
> Where the fountain still is flowing,

And a city is fast growing,
Won and wed our Minnehaha,
Won and wed this beauteous maiden.[20]

The spring featured in Ezra Pound's poem continues to gush. In 1987 Minneapolis hydrologists tested the water and maintained that its natural purity has remained constant for a hundred years. The springs are created by a Cambrian sandstone formation deposited in a marine environment 500 to 570 million years ago. The sandstone at Chippewa Springs is a porous rock material composed mostly of quartz, which naturally filters and stores groundwater as it travels under artesian pressure toward the Chippewa River. The recharge or catchment area for the springs has been identified and protections are in place to safeguard the quality of the water.[21]

The pure water was perfect for making beer. Jacob Leinenkugel arrived in the falls in 1867 with his German recipe for beer.[22] These days the roads leading to Chippewa Falls also guide you to Leinie Lodge and Brewery. I visited the brewery in 2015 for a tour and returned later for an interview with the company's president, Dick Leinenkugel, great-great-grandson of Jacob. Dick succeeded his brother Jake as president. I met with Dick in his office at Leinie Lodge, which is lined with family photos that show the role of family tradition in the company. When I had visited the lodge in February, it seemed to have fewer than ten visitors. This day there must have been two hundred. When I commented on the crowd in the lodge, he told me it has 110,000 visitors each year, 65,000 of whom tour the brewery.

A small family business it is not, especially since Miller Brewing Company in Milwaukee purchased Leinenkugel in 1988. Later, Miller merged with Coors, becoming Miller/Coors. The resources of its parent company have helped Leinenkugel's survive into its sixth generation, and the Leinenkugel family has stayed on running the local operation.[23] On his way to the presidency, Dick worked in the brewery, where he sold and delivered beer. I asked him if his father, Bill, had given him guidance on his path to being a custodian of the business. He said he learned by watching his dad: how concerned he was with taking care of his customers and producing quality beer. A few years back, Dick, Jake, and Bill toured Germany to scout for new ideas and discovered a beer that had a lemonade flavor. They brought that idea home and began testing. They brewed some samples and took them to bars for tasting. When they were satisfied that they had a taste that would please customers, they came out with Summer Shandy. It was an immediate hit. Summer Shandy is brewed only five months a year but outsells all their other kinds of beer.[24]

Like the success of its local brew, Chippewa Falls has much to celebrate: Fur Trade Days recognizes its early heritage, Pure Water Days pays tribute to the quality of its water, and the Northern Wisconsin State Fair provides an opportunity to show off the best of its agricultural resources. But I found the allure of Chippewa Falls goes deeper than its most celebrated claims to fame. Quite simply, it is a place where people come and stay. Sometimes it takes an outsider to recognize that quality in a place. Dave Gordon, president of the Chippewa County Historical Society, arrived after a managerial career in Cincinnati and as a newcomer wondered why so many businesses stay in Chippewa.[25] Skip August, a retired engineer from Cray Research, shared his theory with me: "People fall in love with this place and don't want to leave."[26]

I found that to be true for myself, but it was time to move downriver. We paddled under the Highway 53 bridge headed for Eau Claire.

～

CHAPTER TEN

The Sounds of Summer

Eau Claire

Sometimes we'd have the whole river to ourselves for a long time. . . . Every now and then you'd hear the sounds of a fiddle or a song drifting out across the water from another boat. Then there was the sky, all speckled with stars. We used to lie on our backs and look up at them.

—MARK TWAIN, *THE ADVENTURES OF HUCKLEBERRY FINN*

After several hours on the river from Chippewa Falls, we arrived at the Dells Pond in Eau Claire. The twin steeples of Sacred Heart Church, built in 1928, seem to guard the pond and announce the city. Created by the Dells Dam, the 622-acre lake got its name from the high-banked sandstone dells that line this part of the river.[1] We pushed ashore at Mount Simon Park. While Chippewa Falls has a population exceeding thirteen thousand, Eau Claire has around sixty-six thousand residents and is the education, health, and economic center of the Chippewa River Valley. Once known as "sawdust city," Eau Claire was born in the lumbering days, like many smaller towns up and down the Chippewa.

The steamboat Ida Campbell *can be seen docked at Water Street. Built in Durand, it was the last steamboat to have docked in Eau Claire in about 1882.* CHIPPEWA VALLEY MUSEUM

Prime river territory during the logging era was any place that logs could be stored while awaiting their turn at the mills after their trip downriver. Half Moon Lake, an ancient oxbow of the meandering Chippewa that had long been cut off by erosion, seemed an ideal holding pond. In 1857, a canal was built to link the lake to the Chippewa, and for decades Half Moon Lake served as the primary holding area. After the canal was built, the city rose up as one of the largest milling centers in the state and an economic center of the valley. About twenty wood-processing operations and sawmills sprang up on the shores of the Eau Claire and Chippewa Rivers and Half Moon Lake. The firms included Daniel Shaw, Ingram and Kennedy, Smith and Buffington, and Badger State Lumber, among others.[2] Doug Faulkner, a professor at the

University of Wisconsin–Eau Claire, maintains that the city laid claim to the most prolific sawmills in Wisconsin for half a century.

From the early 1860s on, some in Eau Claire wanted to build a dam at the dells to create another holding pond, but their neighbors to the north in Chippewa Falls objected. The citizens there feared that a dam downriver would obstruct the flow of sawed lumber from their own very large mill. Permission to build the dam had to be granted by the state legislature. As the issue was debated at the capitol in Madison, politicians from Chippewa Falls—including Thaddeus Pound—managed to block the dam for sixteen years. Finally Eau Claire found a way. Eau Claire representatives argued that they needed a dam to supply the city with drinking water, and this argument won the day. In the 1875 session, while Pound happened to be away, the Assembly passed the bill forty-four to thirty-six, and the Senate fifteen to nine.[3]

Completed in 1878, the dam was constructed of oak, timber, sheet iron, concrete, and rock fill. It spanned 428 feet across the river at a height of 19 feet from the bed of the river and a width of 108 feet at its base. In the east end was a sluiceway 10 feet wide for water to run to the community water supply. Next to it was a lock that had a chamber 40 feet wide and 272 feet long. A hinged apron at the lower end of the slide could be adjusted to raise or lower the water to allow traffic through. A wooden flume on the west end headed to Half Moon Lake, running above and along the river, with a walkway for workers to unjam the logs. About halfway to the lake, the logs dropped eighteen feet into a concrete tunnel, which carried the logs the rest of the way underground. This flume and tunnel replaced the 1857 canal as a way to transport logs and lumber between the bodies of water.[4] An engineering marvel, it became a tourist attraction. According to the historical marker that marks its previous location, locals also made use of the channel, from housewives doing laundry to mill workers bathing. After the mills closed, the flume rotted and the tunnel deteriorated until it was sealed and forgotten.[5]

In late December of 1988, Roger and Darlene Regez found out about the tunnel the hard way, when the basement floor of their home on Randall Street collapsed. The house had been built directly over the tunnel. When several other houses built on the disintegrating tunnel also experienced problems, the city decided to purchase the properties and fill the tunnel.[6]

We prepared to re-enter the river below the modern Dells Dam, built in 1924 one hundred feet downstream, drowning the original dam underwater behind it.[7] In 2003 Xcel Energy purchased it from the city. It is the smallest hydro plant on the Chippewa and also the last dam on the river. From here the water flows unobstructed for sixty miles to the Mississippi—the longest unimpeded stretch on the river.

As KC and I looked for a place to put in our canoe, a huge rush of water poured from the dam. This would not be the day to slide old red down the rocky bank into the wild river. We decided to try farther downstream, below the tennis courts at Owen Park.

Half Moon Lake partially surrounds the 134-acre Carson Park, named after lumber baron William Carson.[8] Carson Park is the home of the Eau Claire Cavaliers and at one time the Eau Claire Bears, a farm team of the Milwaukee Braves. This is where Hank Aaron broke into baseball in 1952. When he arrived at the Eau Claire airport carrying a cardboard suitcase, his sole greeter was a sports reporter from the local paper. He had come to play shortstop. In that year, Aaron hit .336 with nine home runs and was selected as Rookie of the Year for the Northern League.[9] In 1955 he was promoted to the Milwaukee Braves.[10] April of 1974 he broke Babe Ruth's home-run record when he banged number 715 over the wall in Atlanta.[11] He returned to Eau Claire on August 17, 1994, to dedicate a statue of himself as a young player, his bat on his shoulder looking out at his future. More than five thousand

The Hank Aaron statue at Carson Park Stadium. RICHARD D. CORNELL

people greeted him that day. Regarding that experience he said, "A lot of things have happened to me in my twenty-three years as a ball player, but nothing touched me more than that day in Eau Claire."[12]

Eau Claire's baseball history goes back much further, to 1867 when the Clearwater Boys played the first organized game of baseball in town.[13] The game moved to Carson Park when it was completed in 1937 at a cost of sixty thousand dollars. While the official capacity was listed at 1,500, about 3,000 came out for the first game between the Bears and Superior Blues.[14] "From 1933 to 1962 minor league professional baseball was Eau Claire's favorite pastime, drawing hundreds of thousands of fans," according to sports historian Jerry Poling.[15]

The Cavaliers have been playing at Carson Park since 1971. When the founders met at Sammy's Pizza to name the team, they

Paul Bunyan and his blue ox at the Paul Bunyan Logging Camp Museum.
RICHARD D. CORNELL

talked about wanting a name for the new team that would reflect the city's French history. That's how they arrived at Cavaliers, a word that derives from the French word for soldiers. They received permission from the Cleveland Cavaliers to use a similar logo.[16] In 2005, Eau Claire Express of the Northwoods League joined the Cavs at Carson Field. The Express built a modern fan deck in right field, and the fans responded by showing up in droves.[17] When either of the hometown teams play on a summer evening, the air hums with the sound of baseball: the smack of a bat, the cheer of the crowd. This is a field of dreams where young players follow their passion with an energy that's not unlike the big leagues.

The drive around Carson Park took us to Paul Bunyan Logging Camp Museum, which preserves remnants of the logging life, including a replica of a bunkhouse. Next door is the Chippewa Valley Museum, which elegantly captures the history of the valley, from the lives of Native peoples and early farmers to medical issues and technology through the years. From the front steps of the museum looking eastward across Half Moon Lake, a large building of the Mayo Clinic Health System can be seen rising into the sky. Originally Luther Hospital built in 1908 by Norwegian ministers, the 304-bed hospital merged with Mayo in 1992. Eau Claire also is home to Sacred Heart Hospital, Marshfield Clinic, and Oak Leaf Surgical Hospital, making it the health care center of the Chippewa Valley.[18]

The street going out of Carson Park leads to Fifth Street and then to Grand Avenue, which heads back to the river. Grand Avenue goes past the location of the old Eau Claire High School, which Saul Brackett attended before his death in the Little Falls tragedy of 1905. In front of the Grand Avenue Café, where I set up a makeshift office to take notes, I could see the Chippewa twinkling in the sun.

On this day, five older folks were gathered at the café for their morning coffee. I decided to ask them a question Adam Cahow had once posed about the city's active music scene: what keeps the music flowing through Eau Claire? One immediately credited the university. Another said it was the location on a popular rail line that cemented the city's music scene. A passenger train called the 400—so-called because it took four hundred minutes to get from Chicago to St. Paul—stopped in Eau Claire, making it accessible to musicians and music lovers alike. Another had a simpler explanation: the people of Eau Claire love music and are an appreciative audience. Still another mentioned Fournier's Ballroom.[19]

Founded in 1950s by French immigrant Wenceslas Fournier, Fournier's Ballroom once hosted nationally known performers such as Louis Armstrong and Buddy Holly. Holly, Richie Valens, and J. P. Richardson (known as the Big Bopper) performed at Fournier's on January 26, 1959, as part of the Winter Dance Party tour.[20] Following their performance, they dined at Sammy's Pizza two blocks from the Eau Claire Hotel where they were staying. A week later, all three died in a plane crash following a performance in Clear Lake, Iowa.[21] Some say the music died that day, but not in Eau Claire.

Another landmark of the local music scene can be found on Water Street. It is one of the oldest buildings on the street, its brick exterior nameless but recognizable to those who know it as the Joynt. Longtime owner Bill Nolte bought the place in 1973, and in 2015 its importance to the local jazz scene earned it a designation as a historical site by the Eau Claire Landmarks Commission. Bill's love of music and his contacts in the music industry enabled him to lure noted musicians on their way to or from the Twin Cities.

In 1974, Bill was listening to a tune on the jukebox when he began to wonder what it would take to attract that particular artist to his saloon, as he calls it. He had a friend who had experience booking artists and together they invited jazz artist Ahmad Jamal, who played at the Joynt on January 21, 1974. That was the beginning of Eau Claire's introduction to the some of the top names in music, as Bill took advantage of his saloon's prime location between Chicago and the Twin Cities.

On May 30, 1976, Duke Ellington's son Mercer, who had taken over his father's orchestra after Duke died, played at the Joynt in between appearances at Orchestra Hall in Minneapolis and Lambeau Field in Green Bay. In 1983 folk singer Odetta performed. After the Joynt, she was headed to Alaska and wanted a warmer coat, so Bill took her to a western wear shop in town. After talking to the clerk, Odetta bought a coat and they left. Back in the car, Bill remembers asking Odetta if she was treated differently, and

Bill Nolte, owner of the Joynt. RICHARD D. CORNELL

she said no. "I said to her, 'I'll bet you are the first black woman she [the clerk] has ever met, and she dealt with you the same way she would deal with anyone.' That," Bill told me, "is why I love Eau Claire. I could travel anywhere, and I have, but I know if I wait, everyone I want to meet will come to me here. You know that Vernon kid won a Grammy and decided to stay here."[22]

He was talking about Justin Vernon, the local musician who in 2012 broke into the national spotlight with his band Bon Iver. He won two Grammys, one for best new artist and one for best alternative album. As Vernon's fame grew, so did his roots in the Eau Claire area. He built a production studio called April Base outside of town that attracts major performers. In 2011 when a writer for the *New York Times* visited Vernon, he took the reporter on a tour of his favorite local places, which included the Joynt, where Vernon's parents first met. "I'm barely at home enough to enjoy the simple lifestyle that I want to live," Vernon told the writer while driving around. "I want to know every inch of this city rather than getting to know a bunch of inches in any other city."[23]

If the local media would have covered the Buddyrevelles band, the information scene in the valley around Eau Claire might look a lot different today. Nick Meyer's frustration over the lack of coverage of his favorite band resulted in his creation of *Volume One*, a free advertising-based publication that covers entertainment and arts in Eau Claire, Chippewa Falls, and Menomonie. He believed that anyone who claimed that nothing interesting ever happened in Eau Claire had a vision problem. He wanted to help people see.

Nick moved from tiny Elk Mound to the "big city" to attend UW–Eau Claire. He formed a band called Vivian and developed a passion for music and the arts. "The mainstream community doesn't realize how valuable the arts can be economically," Nick told me. "Art can have enormous impact as an engine for economic growth." [24]

Nick and Dale Karls produced the first issue of *Volume One* in November of 2001. The first issue was twenty-four pages with a print run of two thousand copies. The print run has since grown to fourteen thousand copies, and the magazine is distributed in more than three hundred locations reaching forty-five thousand readers. The next step in Nick's vision was to create a store: the Local Store in downtown Eau Claire. It features items created in the area: T-shirts with classic images such as London Square Mall and Walter's beer, books by local authors, and music by local musicians. The first store was a prototype for a larger vision. He has since moved to a larger building a few blocks away, overlooking the Eau Claire River, which he refers to as the Local Store World Headquarters.[25]

Tom Giffey, now managing editor of *Volume One*, has traced the impressive history of Eau Claire's music festivals. After the success of Country Fest in Cadott and the oldies festival Shake,

Rattle, and Roll, Country Jam got its start in Eau Claire in 1990 with performers that included Clint Black, Alan Jackson, and Tammy Wynette. Now fans of just about any kind of music can find what they seek in Eau Claire, home to six major music festivals attracting more than one hundred thousand people from around the country each year. Giffey's own research into what makes Eau Claire synonymous with music roughly matched my brief dinner conversations at the café. It's the location between major cities, the scenery of northern Wisconsin on the river, and the region's love of a good tune.[26]

The sidewalk along the river past Fournier's Ballroom leads to Owen Park, where benches circle the front of the band shell. We can imagine the community band playing a summer concert surrounded by rainbow lights reflected in the river as it flows past. The sidewalk continues south, passing the community tennis courts, to Water Street, where steamboats carrying lumber once docked with Water Street in the background. In her book *Remembering Eau Claire*, longtime resident Doris Arnold recalls Water Street during the late lumber era: "The street enjoyed a colorful past as a main thoroughfare during the lumber industry days. Trolleys ran down the center of Water Street from Ninth Avenue to Fourth Avenue every fifteen minutes from 6AM to midnight."[27]

It was also in this area where Old Abe departed Wisconsin to join the front lines of the Civil War, after being purchased by local resident S. M. Jeffers. Joseph O. Barrett, Old Abe's first biographer, described the scene as a cold rain swept over Eau Claire on September 6, 1861:

The bell rang, the engine sprung to duty, off swung the "Stella Whipple" in a graceful curve, and, just as she reached the current, three cheers from the people on the shore greeted the stalwart band, and hands, throwing kisses, and voices choked by tears gave the patriotic "good by."[28]

I can imagine the sendoff, the din of the storm, the bell, and the cheers raising up into a patriotic tune of sorts. The local militia, the Badgers, were headed off to war.

⁓

On a cold windy autumn day in 2001, KC and I re-entered the river, intending to paddle upriver to the Dells Dam to cover the stretch we had skipped. Looking out at the slow-moving current, we pushed off with confidence but soon realized that the power of the river was stronger than it appeared. For every forward stroke, we were pushed back a stroke. After attempting to make progress for an hour, we gave up. The river is a killer at this point. Many people have lost their lives after jumping in from the University of Wisconsin walk bridge, usually after a night of drinking in the bars along Water Street. The school has erected a sign on the bridge warning people of the dangers.

We returned to the tennis court launch in October of 2002. This time, KC and I were joined by her husband, Matt. KC was five months pregnant and looked beautiful in a powder blue top and shorts. At some point I had mentioned my interest in kayaking to KC and Matt, and so they had rented one for me to try. I squeezed into the dark green thing, sitting flat with my legs stretched out in front of me, and we headed out. It wasn't long before my legs became numb, and I realized that kayaking would not be for me.

We paddled under the university walk bridge where my dream of this project began. We passed the beautiful place where the Little Niagara Creek flowed in through a short waterfall. We slipped along the right bank under the parking lot that used to be for Kerm's Super Foods but now fronts an exercise club

Little Niagara. RICHARD D. CORNELL

and a restaurant. This is a special place for me. During summer droughts when the river was very low, this would be the only place the river flowed. The low water exposed a field of rocks and the only visible water flow was at this point. A little rapids would continue to flow below Little Niagara. When Jonathan Carver paddled through here in 1766, he described the "hard rapids & high ledges of rock on each side."[29] To me this area was part of a thalweg, a German term that describes a line connecting the deepest points along the channel of the river. In deep summer I would sit on this high bank and imagine this place to be the soul of the Chippewa.

Nestled in the bluffs and high banks to our left is the University of Wisconsin–Eau Claire. Founded in 1916 as Eau Claire

State Normal School, a college for aspiring teachers, it now has more than nine thousand students and is rated thirty-third in the nation of the schools of its class.[30] One of the many oaks shading the campus is the Council Oak. The enormous tree served as an important meeting place of the Ojibwe and Dakota, who reached an agreement for peace in the 1850s after a century and a half of fighting over territory. The three-hundred-year-old tree was felled by a windstorm in 1987, but a new oak, donated by Ojibwe tribal elders, was planted in its place.[31]

Higher up the bluff is the Chippewa Valley Technical College (CVTC). With more than three thousand full-time students, it is widely respected for its contribution to the valley. In 2013, I interviewed Jerry Jacobson, president of the Northwestern Bank in Chippewa Falls, while investigating the contribution of Cray Research to the economy of the valley. "Of course Cray was important," Jacobson said, "but there are very few employed people we meet who did not graduate from CVTC."[32]

The school was created in 1911 to provide skill training, carpentry, and mechanical drawing for boys, and cooking and telegraphy for girls. As the skill needs of the valley grew, so did the offerings. In the 1960s, training in comptometers—early mechanical calculators—was provided for employees of U.S. Rubber. "We offered classes that people wanted, the community needed, and employers suggested," Norbert Wurtzel, president of the school from 1974 to 1994, told an interviewer.[33] In the 1970s the school expanded its offerings in adult basic education courses, through which many adults earned their general equivalency diploma or got help for employment or school admission. Today the program is active in teaching English to the many recent immigrants in the valley. Every Tuesday evening during the school year, KC teaches one of those classes. By now an assistant director of instruction at Cooperative Educational Service Agency 10, she feeds her soul by teaching these new arrivals.

~

Galloway Street, the current location of the Local Store, runs along the Eau Claire River a mile or so upstream from its mouth and the confluence with the Chippewa. This stretch on the north bank of the Eau Claire has been the center of dynamic economic activity for more than a hundred years.

During the lumber era, this spot was home to the largest lumber mill in the city. Union Lumber was purchased by Frederick Weyerhaeuser and became the Mississippi River Logging Company (MRL Co.).[34] *The Business Atlas of the City of Eau Claire of 1888* shows the MRL Co.'s place along the river. Just upstream was the McDonough's Foundry. An ad in the atlas features "Frank McDonough Manufacturing of Saw Mill Machinery."[35] The company still exists, making it the longest-running business in Eau Claire. Now called simply McDonough, it has relocated to near the Chippewa Valley Regional Airport. In 2015 Jerry Price and I visited McDonough Vice President Matt Tietz and his mother, Susan, the company's president. Matt showed us the high-tech manufacturing process, which builds the automated log-processing equipment the company sells around the world.[36]

The last lumber moved down the Chippewa in 1912. In 1916, the Gillette Safety Tire Company was built in the general area of the former MRL Co. Mill. This went on to become U.S. Rubber, which was taken over by the US government during World War II for the manufacture of small-caliber munitions. In August of 1943, the plant was released and converted to tire production. U.S. Rubber doubled the size of the plant in 1947 and increased employment from prewar levels to forty-four hundred. By 1951 the plant was the fifth largest tire plant in the country. After several changes in ownership, the plant, by then called Uniroyal, closed in 1991.[37] After ninety years the vital place of employment along the north shore of the Eau Claire River fell silent. The 11.9

Bill and Patti Cigan at their home on the Chippewa.
COURTESY OF PATRICIA M. CIGAN

million-square-foot brick structure stood empty. Now the only sound was the music of the rapids in the Eau Claire River and an occasional car along Galloway Street. It waited for Bill Cigan.

Bill was both a dreamer and an achiever. After service in the US Navy in World War II, he returned to Eau Claire and received a teaching degree from UW–Eau Claire. But teaching made him restless, so he got a job selling candy and toys for a Chicago firm. He had found his dream job—salesman. From there he began his own vending machine company, Variety Vending, in 1958. In 1978 he imagined a way to sell snacks at very small businesses that couldn't afford to have a vending machine. He used cardboard trays and sold on the honor system, calling it the Honor Shoppe. The word of this innovation got out, and NBC's *Today Show* featured him in two segments in 1982.[38]

Sometime after Uniroyal closed, Bill called his wife, Patti, and stepson, Jack Kaiser, into his office. "I want to buy the old Uniroyal Plant," he said. And they did.[39] They called it Banbury after a tire-manufacturing device. Today the multiuse facility houses 130 retail and small-manufacturing units. According to Chamber CEO Bob McCoy, Bill envisioned Banbury as one giant business incubator.[40] It has achieved that goal. Jack Kaiser described the growth of two renters: Goldstar Tech expanded from occupying six hundred square feet to twenty-seven thousand square feet with fifteen employees, and Steel Toe Shoes grew from six hundred square feet to twenty-one thousand square feet, also with fifteen employees.[41]

Growth and innovation like this has expanded employment opportunities, kept people living in the valley, and attracted newcomers. This in turn has translated to support for the arts community. After years of trying to make a performing arts center happen at the confluence of the Chippewa and Eau Claire, in 2014 local leaders started moving on the Confluence Project. The development will include the arts center, apartments, and a public plaza.

The sounds along the Chippewa have come a long way since Eau Claire's early days as a logging town. The logs and lumber of the white pine that floated on the river have been replaced by the lazy laughter of today's visitors who launch their tubes and other floating craft from Phoenix Park and float under the university walk bridge enjoying a summer day. On a summer evening it swirls past a concert at Phoenix Park at the confluence with the Eau Claire River. These concerts are the result of a vision Nick Meyer had one winter day while driving past the park. Less than a mile downstream, tunes from individual performers and a community band drift from the band shell at Owen Park. Five miles downstream at various times in the summer, a hammering bluegrass band serenades

Music event at Phoenix Park, located at the confluence of the Chippewa and Eau Claire Rivers. ANDREA PAULSETH/VOLUME ONE

the water, and later the strum of a country guitar hangs in the twilight.

Back on the river, we paddled under the West Clairemont Avenue Bridge and entered the Lower Chippewa.

~

CHAPTER ELEVEN

A Storybook Ending

The Lower Chippewa

All girt about with circling hills
And wooded slopes on every hands—
Our little city of Durand.
—ELIZABETH CLARKE HARDY, POET

I've heard various opinions on what constitutes the Lower Chippewa. The Lower Chippewa Alliance defines it as the sixty-one miles from the Dells Dam in Eau Claire to the Mississippi. Xcel Energy interprets it as where the Flambeau enters above the small town of Holcombe. In 2010, the Wisconsin DNR began a study of the Lower Chippewa where the Red Cedar enters. Doug Faulkner of UW–Eau Claire claims it begins below Jim Falls. For me the Lower Chippewa starts at the first island below the West Clairemont Avenue Bridge in Eau Claire. It is here that the river begins to look the way it does for the next sixty miles, resembling the Mississippi more than its upper stretches, with many meanders, islands, and sand—lots of sand.

Below Eau Claire, the river's last sixty miles have been set free. It has flowed past eight towns, spun turbines in eight power plants, embraced many tributaries, and now on its way to the

Mississippi, it runs unimpeded, sliding past many islands and carrying tons of sand to the big river. It is wide and powerful. The flow at Bishops Bridge below the Winter Dam is around 714 CFS; at Durand it's 7,638.[1] The amount of sand this water carries into the mouth creates a challenge for the US Army Corps of Engineers, which maintains a nine-foot channel to maintain traffic flow on the Mississippi.

In addition to a whole lot of sand, this stretch carries the stories of famous literary figures, gunfights and murder, ghost towns, wars over lumber rights, and steamboats. KC and I paddled the sixty miles of wide, lazy river from Eau Claire to Mississippi in three days; we were largely unaware of the surrounding tales. I returned over the course of three months to learn their details. The stories live on in the memory of custodians of the river: a retired farmer and his son, who makes historical films about the Chippewa; a UW–Eau Claire professor who moonlights as a cartographer of the river; a retired research engineer who preserves the last boat landing before the Mississippi; and countless others.

Our journey once again began in Eau Claire. On its west bank below the West Clairemont Bridge is Shawtown, a collection of modest homes and businesses. Caradori Pottery now stands in the onetime location of lumberman Daniel Shaw's home. David Caradori was studying nursing at UW–Eau Claire when he signed up for what he thought would be an easy elective: pottery. He took to the craft more than he ever expected and has been working the potter's wheel for the past forty years. While I chatted with him in his shop, he explained the various pots: an assortment of functional and specialty pieces fired in the reduction gas kiln in-shop or in a wood-burning kiln located about ten miles away. Caradori also features work by a number of other local artists. David showed me a couple of items by Laurie Bieze, a revered local stained-glass artist who died of cancer on June 22, 2014. "I don't know any person who has done more for the arts in Eau

David Caradori, artist and owner of Caradori Pottery. RICHARD D. CORNELL

Claire than Laurie," David told me. "She was so encouraging to people and was instrumental in building the local art community." When she developed cancer, he accompanied her to the doctor and listened as she demanded to know the truth about her condition. Her life motto was "To thine own self be true." He and others have been lobbying for a gallery to be named after her in the new building at the confluence.[2]

On this upper part of the lower river, you can look up and see the giant Silver Mine Hill ski jump. Each February, it's the site of an Eau Claire competition that dates back 130 years and draws flyers from Canada, Norway, Finland, Slovenia, and—of course—the local ski club, the Flying Eagles. The ninety-foot scaffold was built in Indiana in 1927 and moved to the hill overlooking the Chippewa.[3] On a cold January weekend in 2015, two of KC's boys, Logan and Stewart, were among the competitors. KC stood in the

The Silver Mine Hill ski jump. RICHARD D. CORNELL

freezing wind, terrified of her boys muffing the tall jump, but they both sailed through the air and stuck their landings.

In June and July along this stretch, you can hear the strains of the music festivals along the west bank. On the east bank, bicyclists pedal by on the Chippewa River bike trail. The thirty-mile trail begins at Phoenix Park and ends at Durand. It follows the bed of the Milwaukee Road Line built in 1882.[4]

When Samuel Clemens was training to become a riverboat pilot, he had to memorize the Mississippi, learning how all its currents and details changed with the weather and the seasons. The steamboat captains who navigated the Chippewa in the mid- to late 1800s had the same charge. Those boats pushed lumber and log rafts to the Mississippi. They carried passengers to and from the railhead at Reads Landing across the Mississippi in Minnesota.

When the river is low, evidence of mankind's attempts to control it appears. Cribs were built and filled with rocks as a way of guiding the river into the main channel to support floating lumber and log rafts. How they managed to pound posts the size of telephone poles deep enough into the riverbed to hold it all together when the floods came is a mystery to me. And the floods did come. In 1880, spring rains brought the river up twenty-three feet, washing out most of the mills in Chippewa and Eau Claire. In 1884 the Chippewa rose again. Each time, the waters downriver flowed wild, refusing to be penned. The last big flood occurred in 1941, a distant memory as KC and I paddled the wide lazy river south of Eau Claire. Downriver from Eau Claire we paddled under the next bridge at Caryville.

In 1886 Caryville, located on the south side of the Chippewa, had a feed mill, a pickle factory, and a post office. In 1901 a ferry, powered by a Model A engine, was built to provide transportation to farmers on the south side. It was so used, it was considered an extension of the road.[5] Jim Alf, in his seventies when I talked to him, began working the ferry, which operated from early March to late November, when he was twelve years old. Peak traffic, according to Alf, was Sunday when up to three hundred cars crossed the river. Jim ended his ferry days in 1964 when the bridge was built. For a number of years he served area farmers with a portable sawmill, turning round things into flat things. Eventually he gave that up for health reasons and drove a semi cross-country for eight years; his wife, Karen, was co-driver for three years. In retirement, they live in a small condo near the Eau Claire public soccer field, and Jim is a leader in the local writing community.[6]

KC and I passed Brush Island, then Happy Island, the home of the old town of Meridean. While researching I came across the legend of the Meridean boat landing—supposedly haunted

Brian Gabriel, Lower Chippewa historian and filmmaker. RICHARD D. CORNELL

by Meridean herself. Meridean died aboard a riverboat and was buried in the area, and according to local lore, her ghost now tries to lure others to share her fate.[7] I asked Brian Gabriel, a retired farmer who is fluent in the area's history, what he made of the story. Brian believes the Meridean ghost stories to be a total fabrication conceived by people trying to make a name for themselves. Jim Alf thinks that drug dealers in the area saw the "ghosts."

Brian grew up on a small farm that bordered the river. He recalls looking out of his bedroom window when he was five and seeing mallard ducks swimming in his front yard. The river had flooded the property. Brian later bought the farm from his father and continued to deal with the whims of the rising and receding waters. Once he left a field full of baled hay for a weekend vacation with his family. When he returned, the bales had disappeared. In his absence the river had risen, seizing the bales in its currents, and carried them off downriver.

The Gabriel farm was down a gravel road from New Meridean. At the end of the logging era, the town had moved to the mainland. New Meridean, according to Brian, had everything a person could want: "You could go to church, attend school, get your car fixed, buy groceries, everything a family would need." When the railroad stopped running, New Meridean faded. Today all that remains are a few houses and empty storefronts. After years of battling the river on that small farm, Brian gave up his passion for working the land, sold the farm, and moved to Menomonie. A short time after his move, his son Evan talked his dad into making videos covering the history of the lower river. Evan has moved to Kansas, but Brian continues the tradition by keeping people on his mailing list updated with the most recent historical photos and tidbits people have sent him.[8]

On our next trip, we left Meridean and headed for Durand. On the way we hit Chippewa Island, also known as Pasture Island. The river starts to resemble a snake just before passing by the confluence with Red Cedar River. It is in this area, according to Sean Hartnett of the UW–Eau Claire Watershed Institute, that the sand really emerges. Sand banks line the meandering river, pushing tons of sediment toward the Mississippi.

As we traveled downriver, we paddled under what was once a railroad bridge and is now a bicycle trail. We passed Nine Mile Island, went under the Highway 10 bridge, and arrived at Durand, where we stopped for the day.

Of the many towns along the Chippewa, only Durand, Glidden, Cornell, and Eau Claire share such proximity to the water. In this way, Durand is a true river town, much like Hannibal, Missouri, where Samuel Clemens grew up. In *Life on the Mississippi*, the writer who became known as Mark Twain describes his boyhood in Hannibal, painting a picture of lazy summer afternoons with people dozing along the street. Whenever a stream of smoke appeared on the horizon, someone would yell, "Steamboat

Terry Mesch, manager of the Pepin County Old Courthouse Museum and Jail.
RICHARD D. CORNELL

a comin'!" and the town would shake itself awake.[9] This would have been life in Durand in the days when steamboats traveled from Reads Landing to Eau Claire.

One summer day Dixie and I took a trip to Durand for photos. I was walking around with a large Canon camera hanging around my neck when a man in a small red car pulled up alongside. "You don't look like you are from around here," he said. The man was Terry Mesch, director of the history museum in Durand, located in the last remaining wood courthouse in Wisconsin. Terry opened the door and invited us in. Inside, a world of poets, murderers, and a world-class educator would be opened to us. He led me to the following stories.

The most famous name to come out of Pepin County is, of course, Laura Ingalls Wilder. In 1862, her grandparents, parents, and other family members arrived a few miles from Pepin and built a log cabin. Years later the family headed for Minnesota. Laura later described Lake Pepin—the massive lake created in the Mississippi by sand flowing out of the Chippewa—as they crossed it by covered wagon in winter: "The enormous lake stretched flat and smooth and white all the way to the edge of the gray sky."[10]

Laura Ingalls Wilder was in her sixties when she wrote this. She was writing a column on the joys of farm life for the *Missouri Ruralist* when she caught the attention of a publisher who encouraged her to write a column on farm life. Later, she wrote a memoir, *Pioneer Girl*, but no publisher was interested. Her daughter, Rose, a popular writer at the time, encouraged her to reshape the book for children. *Little House in the Big Woods* became a huge hit, and she went on to write ten more books.[11] In 2015 the South Dakota Historical Society Press finally published *Pioneer Girl*, which became a bestseller.

While Laura Ingalls Wilder is a national treasure, another writer had a closer connection to the Lower Chippewa. Elizabeth Clarke Hardy arrived in the Durand area in 1871. For forty years, she and her husband lived on a lovely piece of property they called Springbrook, located on County Road M a few miles east of town. Her poem "The Unknown Shore" was read at the funerals of two American presidents, James Garfield and Woodrow Wilson. She also penned a poem in honor of the town she loved, recounting the many things that made it grand: local landmarks and buildings, nature's majesty in the river and trees, busy streets full of dedicated citizens:

> City of home where peace abides,
> And culture and good cheer abound,
> Where friendship ripened with the years,
> And hospitality are found. [12]

In 1881, when Elizabeth was ten years old, the peace of Durand was shattered by a late-afternoon gunfight that left Charles and Milton Coleman, brothers and honored lawmen of the area, dead. The story of the lynching that followed would haunt the town for years.

The story began with another set of brothers, Ed and Lon Maxwell, who began their life of crime as young boys trying to make easy money in Illinois. Raised in poverty by a strict, religious father, they taught themselves to be crack shots with their Colt Navy revolvers and Winchester rifles. After successfully pulling off a robbery in Stillwater, Minnesota, they escalated to burglary and horse theft, using the alias Williams.

Lon, a more reluctant participant, fell in love with Fannie Husse, and soon they were married and expecting a child. Fannie wasn't aware of her husband's criminal activity until Pepin County Undersheriff Miletus Knight visited her to look for the brothers. The stress of this information possibly brought on an early stillbirth that resulted in her death. On June 26, 1881, Lon wrote a letter to Elder Downer, the minister who had married them: "I want to say that no man was ever more honest in dealing with a woman than I was with her. Circumstances placed me in such position that I could hear nothing of the way things were going up here till I finally came up. But too late, she was dead."[13] Lon was incensed and set out with Ed to find Undersheriff Knight.

One late afternoon in July the brothers ferried across the Chippewa to Durand. As word spread that the notorious Williams brothers were in town, two brothers—Deputy Milton Coleman of Menomonie and Deputy Charles Coleman of Durand—set out to find them. The two pairs of brothers met up at about 8 p.m. where Highway 10 and Highway 85 intersect. In the shootout that followed, the Coleman brothers were both killed, and the Maxwell brothers were wounded. Lon had significant

The old Pepin County Courthouse building, where Ed Maxwell would have been tried, served as the county courthouse from 1873 to 1985 and is now a museum.
RICHARD D. CORNELL

buckshot wounds to his left arm and shoulder, but the two men managed to escape on a stolen boat on the Chippewa.

Bloodhounds and up to five hundred men, including Indian trackers and members of the Menomonie Ludington Guard, pursued the brothers. On November 9, the posse caught up to them at a farm near Grand Island, Nebraska. Sheriff Joseph Killian of Hall County, Nebraska, arrested Ed. Lon escaped and was never seen again. Ed was taken to St. Paul, Minnesota, where a thousand people gawked at him at the train station. From there he was moved to Menomonie, where the Coleman brothers' mother confronted him. "Why did you kill my boys?" she asked, to which Ed replied, "We didn't know who they were and they fired on us first."[14] Ed had planned on pleading self-defense during the trial, but the trial never took place. On November 19, Ed was brought to the Pepin County Courthouse in Durand for a preliminary hearing, as hundreds of people gathered in the streets. Before the proceedings began, a group of about fifteen men grabbed Ed, dragged him from the courthouse, and hanged him from a tree. The lynching in Durand caught the attention of the national news with major coverage by the *New York Times* and other papers.[15]

The incident was a blemish on the history of a town with its share of more respectable claims to fame. Twelve years following the lynching of Ed Williams, Helen Parkhurst graduated from Durand High School. She would have a significant impact on elementary education in America. After attending college at River Falls, she began her teaching career on the Chippewa at Black School, a one-room school near Arkansaw, Wisconsin. From there she moved to UW–Stevens Point, where she headed up the elementary education program. In 1913, she went to Italy, where she met Maria Montessori, a pioneer in student-led education for students of a range of abilities. As a result of that friendship and their shared view of education, Montessori asked Parkhurst to be her representative in the United States. After years of working for the Montessori program, Parkhurst developed her ideas and founded the first Dalton School in New York City based on her philosophy.

> [In many traditional classrooms], sharp children are held
> back and dull children are pushed on, to the detriment of
> their mental powers, owing to the teacher's effort to strike the
> problematical average.... [And] how many class lessons have
> children to listen to which are boring and useless, and others
> where they are not sufficiently interested to ask a question?
> If we use class teaching and individual work in their proper
> places, the best results will follow.[16]

The only Dalton School remaining in the United States is in New York, but about four hundred are located in the Netherlands, where Parkhurst is a national hero.

During the logging era of the 1800s, the Chippewa River divided in two as it neared the Mississippi. One branch was the main channel, the other a long, slow-moving pool that at first flowed parallel to the main channel but eventually joined the Mississippi near Alma, Wisconsin.[17] This second branch—which came to be known as Beef Slough—was perfect for log storage. In 1867 a consortium from Michigan and Wisconsin called Beef Slough Company developed a plan to make log rafts to float logs to the mills down the Mississippi.[18] The twenty-some mills in Eau Claire opposed the diversion of logs away from their own operations to the Slough. In 1868, James "Beef Slough" Bacon led 150 armed men upriver to confront the Eau Claire mill owners.[19] They cut a number of booms, allowing millions of feet of logs to float downriver. This came to be known as the lumber war on the Chippewa, and it was a boon to the communities downriver. In that same year, explorer C. H. Cooke returned from his canoe adventure and observed the following: "A local or home interest made me glad that Eau Claire had been beaten in trying to monopolize the logging business. These logs were to be rafted and sorted and all business touching them done in my hometown of Alma. I was glad of it."[20]

Four years later, thirty-eight-year-old German immigrant Frederick Weyerhaeuser was elected president of the Mississippi River Logging Company. He convinced the warring parties of the advantages of working together, thus creating an economic advantage over mills located elsewhere on the river.

❧

On July 31, 2003, we slid our canoe into the Chippewa at Durand for the fifteen-mile journey that would conclude our trip. KC was five months pregnant. Her husband, Matt, saw us off with a warning: "Don't go under any bridges." The only bridge we might go under would be Highway 35, the railroad bridge just before entering the Mississippi. Matt didn't want his wife to enter the big river, so he planned to pick us up at the bridge.

It was my sixtieth birthday, and KC had brought a cake. A few miles downriver on the north side, we reached the boat landing at Ella and enjoyed the cake at a picnic table. Ella, also known as Shoo-fly, is the last landing on the Chippewa, seven miles above the Mississippi.

In 1854, this was the site of one of many bloody skirmishes in the later years of feuding between the Dakota and the Ojibwe. According to LCO educator and historian Rick St. Germaine, Ojibwe headman Nenaangebi and other members of his hunting party were killed by the Dakota in an ambush along the Hay River south of Prairie Farm. The Dakota attacked to avenge the killing of their own hunters by the Ojibwe two years before at Battle Island, south of Durand on the Chippewa River. The victors displayed Nenaangebi's scalp the next day at Shoo-fly.[21]

The Ojibwe and Dakota had been warring intermittently for hundreds of years by that point, as growing populations, scarce natural resources, and pressure from white settlement pushed them into each other's territories. The area around the mouth of the Chippewa was the site of some of the most vicious fighting between the two tribes. In the summer of 1795, an Ojibwe war chief known as Big Ojibway set out down the river with a war party of twenty- three warriors to avenge the killing of some of his relatives. When they arrived at the mouth of the Chippewa they saw a large band of Dakotas camped across the river. Beating drums sounded as they prepared to go on the warpath. According to Ojibwe historian William Warren, "The Ojibway war party laid an ambush at a spot peculiarly adapted for the purpose, by a thick forest of trees which grew to the very banks of the Chippeway River." The next morning two hundred Dakota warriors began to paddle up the Chippewa, and the Ojibwe attacked, killing several Dakota headmen. The Ojibwe assumed with the loss of their leaders the Dakota would retreat, but instead the Dakota came ashore. Big Ojibway, a heavy man who could not run far himself, ordered the rest of his men to run; he would hold off the Dakota. According to Warren's version of the story, the Dakota found him calmly sitting in a clump of grass in a small prairie smoking his pipe. Fearing an ambush, they surrounded him and waited. When they decided he was alone, they shot him. Wounded, Big Ojibway rose up laughing and yelling and charged with his spear, wounding several before he died. The Dakota then cut out Big Ojibway's heart; each ate a piece of it in honor of his bravery and believing they would acquire some of his courage in this way.[22]

Long after the Ojibwe and Dakota stopped fighting, the land of this area is still considered precious. In April 2012, I boarded the Chippewa Valley Motor Car train for a five-mile journey to explore the Tiffany Wildlife Area. The train runs along an abandoned Milwaukee rail line that has been leased to a group of rail buffs by Xcel Energy for a dollar a year. Mike Hogseth of the Wisconsin Department of Natural Resources was our guide. He described the Tiffany as a floodplain ecosystem, a patchwork of different habitats comprising bottomland hardwood forest. It is the largest floodplain forest in the upper Midwest, approximately fifteen thousand acres at the mouth of the Chippewa River, right before it reaches its confluence with the Mississippi. Because it's so gigantic, it offers a very good habitat for bird species that require a lot of space to roam, such as cerulean warblers and Kentucky warblers. It also has possibly the last strong population of the massasauga rattlesnake, which overwinters alongside streambeds.

Several miles above Durand, the Lower Chippewa River Alliance worked with Xcel Energy to restore the four-thousand-acre Tyrone land. Xcel acquired the land in the 1960s and 1970s as a potential nuclear generating site, but the plant was never built.[23] After thirty years of misuse as an ATV playground and dumping site, Xcel funded cleanup efforts, with the alliance providing volunteer labor. In 2007, Xcel partnered with the Wisconsin DNR on restoration projects for the savannahs and grasslands. The state was considering purchase of the land as of 2016.[24]

I met Carl Morsbach at the meeting of the Lower Chippewa River Alliance on July 28, 2014. He introduced himself as the mayor of Ella. Carl told me that if I went to the Shoo-fly Landing on the river and looked up, I would see his house. On August 22, Jerry Price and I paid him a visit. We could barely see his house through the dense trees. The only visible business in Ella is an auto repair garage where there always seems to be someone with his head under a raised car hood.

We drove up a narrow winding road that had been washed out in places by rushing water. The house was sort of white but in need of painting. Sagging screens graced the windows on the second floor. A number of scrapped cars were partially hidden in tall grass.

Four dogs rushed out and surrounded our car. We decided to wait for Carl to appear. After quite a while, a woman emerged, scolding the dogs, followed by Carl. When Carl came up to the car, I got out and shook his hand. One of the dogs nipped me on the back of my leg, and the woman grumbled something to Carl about what she would like to do with that dog. "It's okay," Carl reassured her. "He doesn't know him yet. Look, he already smells something good on him." Carl assured me the dog and I would be friends just as soon as he got to know me. I petted him and he looked up at me with suspicious eyes.

As we stood outside, I asked Carl why the boat landing was called Shoo-fly. He wasn't sure, but he said he heard once that passing paddleboats often saw women on the shore shooing flies away.

Ella is seven miles from the Mississippi and eight miles from Durand. Ella had a hotel during the logging days, according to Carl. Men who had guided lumber rafts downriver would walk back to Eau Claire, stopping halfway to rest overnight. Today the river is for canoeing, kayaking, and tubing, and most river travelers bypass Ella to take out at the Highway 35 bridge.

Before ending up in Ella, Carl had various engineering jobs—mechanical, electrical, civil. He worked at General Dynamics Atlas Missile base in Nebraska and spent fifteen years in advanced development at Honeywell in Minneapolis. At other times, he worked in Texas and Florida. As we talked, I looked at his wife, Patricia, who had planted herself in a metal chair to listen in, and asked her if she was with him on all of these travels. "Oh, yes, with Carl you never know what will happen, but it will be interesting." They had been married for thirty-three years.

After retiring in 2000, Carl returned to Ella to take over the family farm. He traces his ancestry to two brothers who emigrated from Germany in 1847. His great-grandfather was a pharmacist in Durand. The other brother went to Oregon state and fought in the Mexican-American War, which earned him the rights to a land claim.

I asked about Five-Mile Bluff, which overlooks the Chippewa and Mississippi within Tiffany Wildlife Area. Carl told me I'd have a much better view in the hills above where we were standing. He called the hilltop a "goat prairie," a southern-facing hill that has its own ecology. He said the area was once an oak savannah.

Carl said the boat landing at Ella is in jeopardy because of sand buildup. The meandering Lower Chippewa scoops the sandy banks and transports the sand downriver, most of it ending up in the Mississippi. When the Chippewa reaches the Mississippi, it is eight feet higher than the big river. It was this flow of sand that penned the river, creating Lake Pepin, which at one time extended all the way to St. Paul.[25]

In 1939 the Army Corps of Engineers was tasked with the job of maintaining a nine-foot channel in the Mississippi to maintain barge travel for cargo such as grain and coal. In 1984, the Corps built a sand trap to reduce the amount of sediment flowing from the Chippewa into the Mississippi. The trap succeeded in a 40 percent reduction.[26]

In the summer of 2014 Dixie and I drove to Reads Landing to observe the mouth of the Chippewa. From across the Mississippi below Lake Pepin, the mouth appears small, and below the mouth we saw mounds of sand. A bit downstream in the Mississippi, a boat was dredging sand from the river.

Ten thousand years ago the roaring Chippewa dammed up the Mississippi and formed Lake Pepin. It remains a problem to this day.

⌁

We pushed off from the Ella landing for the final leg of our journey. Behind us were many memories: The night we slept on the small island on the East Fork. The day KC, Brian, and I pushed off below the Winter Dam, the formal start of the river. The night we spotted the Pabst Blue Ribbon sign in front of Boggie's Bar as we paddled in the dark. I watched KC, my daughter carrying her own unborn child, dig in with her paddle, her head bowed into a gentle breeze. Was the ghost of Big Ojibway watching as we paddled past the Tiffany Wildlife Area?

The last days on the river were difficult. KC was frustrated with me for the many times I canceled a trip. Once she said she would finish the trip alone. Later she told me she had been complaining to her hairdresser about my procrastination. "Don't you understand," the stylist told KC, "he doesn't want to finish it."

As we approached the landing below the Highway 35 bridge, several fish jumped out of the river ahead of us. "Did you see that?" she asked me. "They are celebrating our arrival!" I remembered the two mallards that flew up as we entered Glidden.

The last words in my river journal: "I didn't want this to end."

Epilogue

Eventually, all things merge into one, and a river runs through it. The river was cut by the world's great flood and run over rocks from the basement of time.
— NORMAN MACLEAN, *A RIVER RUNS THROUGH IT*

The story of the Chippewa River tells itself. It begins as two branches, the East Fork and the West Fork, draped like a necklace from below Lake Superior to the Mississippi. They flow together near the small town of Winter, where they are captured by a dam. When you stand on the Winter Dam looking out at the thirteen-thousand-acre Chippewa Flowage, you have to imagine the two forks of the river that once flowed beneath. Looking to your right you can see the East Fork as it ends its independent journey. Looking down from the dam, you can hear and see the white water that rushes out and forms the main Chippewa. From here other than the Arpin Dam near Radisson, it flows free to where it joins the Flambeau River above the Holcombe Flowage.

The story of the Chippewa River is a story of the natural resources that have shaped human history. It carried the wood that built the American towns and cities in the 1800s. It transported fur traders and explorers. Its gifts led to the creation of all the towns that exist along the river today. Electricity from the dams supports thousands of homes and businesses. The water supports wildlife and recreational activities. It is a story of the struggle between humans and nature. It exemplifies the constant trade-off between protecting our natural heritage and supporting human life.

Life along the river has been shaped by societal change and legal struggles. The treaty of 1837 opened the valley to logging, and the river was the key to moving logs to the mills. Numerous legal battles ensued over control of the river by dams, from the Beef Slough war to the Water Power Act of 1920, which opened the way to hydroelectric dams. The dams at Winter, Cornell, and Jim Falls were all built during the twenties as a result.

Sean Hartnett, who is with the UW–Eau Claire Watershed Institute for Collaborative Environmental Studies, uses his Zodiac boat and high-powered sonar to map the rocky bottom of the river. Thanks to him we can see the shape of the wild Chippewa below the dams on bathymetric maps. The old channel at Jim Falls also offers a glimpse of the original wild Chippewa flowing over pre-Cambrian rock. You can witness the river that has flowed for close to ten thousand years. And it grows as it goes along. The average flow four miles below the Winter Dam is six hundred cubic feet per second. At the place where it flows past the Tiffany Wildlife Area a few miles above the Mississippi, it's six thousand cubic feet per second. The pearls of small towns built amidst the white pines adorn its edge. Other than Chippewa Falls and Eau Claire, this is a small-town river.

The true untamed river can still be viewed in many places. The best of these is between the Winter Dam and the point where the Flambeau joins the Chippewa above the Holcombe Flowage. Here you experience nine-mile rapids and the Big Bend as it passes by Flambeau Ridge below Bruce. I recall the night we stopped at the small log-cabin bar a few miles above the Flambeau. I wrote that I thought I could feel the river slow down. "You were right," someone said, "Xcel owns her from here down." Adam Cahow informed me that this part of the river also naturally has a low gradient and slows itself down.

No one can truly own the river. Xcel has to justify its right to dam it every fifty years. In a way, relicensing is a formality because of our dependence on hydroelectric power, but it is also an opportunity for negotiation. The negotiation between the DNR, Ojibwe, Xcel, US Forest Service, and landowners around the Chippewa Flowage resulted in an agreement to protect this great wilderness area more effectively than any law has done.

From the trout streams at the headwaters to the musky pools along the way, the river invites the angler. Every year, hundreds of people float the river in inner tubes unaware of the history they are riding on.

On my own journey, I imagined Old Abe at the Civil War battle at Vicksburg, Mississippi, flying low and screaming over the battle noise as a Confederate officer wished him dead. I pictured a young Hank Aaron proving himself under the lights at Carson Park in Eau Claire. I thought of Charlie Fischer building his resort at Bear Lake, Woody Rawls looking out at the river as he wrote, Seymour Cray moving to Chippewa Falls with his dream of building the world's fastest computer, Bill Nolte bringing big-time musicians to Eau Claire, and Durand with its poets and gunfighters.

A number of sources have told me that in the very early days the Ojibwe would travel down the Chippewa during the warm months, returning to their homes up north when winter set in. The rivers of the valley were their highways, much more central to human life today. I asked Ojibwe elder Dennis Banks how the power-plant dams affected the Chippewa. He said that before the damming, the floods provided natural renewal of the river, reseeding the medicinal plants along its banks each time it flooded. The dams have tamed the river, and taming always reins in wildness.

But the wildness had its downsides. The floods of the Chippewa that happened every few years often washed out sawmills. Doing business on the Chippewa required considerable investment and considerable risk. By reining in nature, we can minimize risk but not eliminate it. Every spring, the river still swells and pushes its way through the dams. It's quite a thing to see.

Once when I came back from a teaching gig in a big city, I returned to Eau Claire to see high, rough water pushing against the bridge and splashing over the bike trail and tennis courts. As Dixie and I walked down to look, she recalled an earlier visit when she had stood next to Eau Claire artist Signe Ortiz and watched a similarly wild river. Ortiz had commented, "Now that's the way it ought to be."

The dams are supposed to tame it, but sometimes the river overcomes them. A print that hangs in my office titled "River Engineering" shows drawings of dams around the world. I keep it there as a reminder that in the long run, the river engineers itself. From Lake Chippewa Flowage to Eau Claire, six power dams grab and then release the river. But dam building didn't begin in modern times; it didn't even begin with humans. The morning Pat Bonney and I looked at the source of the East Fork, which had coalesced as a shimmering pool, Pat speculated that it had been contained by a beaver dam. In logging days, the Chippewa and its tributaries had more than one hundred dams.

This project began for me at the University of Wisconsin–Eau Claire walk bridge. Before canoeing it, I used to muse about the Chippewa and what lay upriver. Dixie and I went to the bridge quite often after we moved to the area, when we crossed it to reach the bike trail along the river, on July 4 to watch the reflection of the fireworks from Carson Park, and in October, when, if we were lucky, we witnessed a convention of hundreds of mallards gathered beneath the bridge.

While I lived near its banks, the river became more visible to me over time. When I moved to Eau Claire in 1976, I hoped to live in a house overlooking Dells Pond. The houses there were lower in cost than neighborhoods away from the river, and I asked my real estate agent why. He said that many residents still think of living along the river as living next to the factory, which is what it was during the lumbering days. Dixie and I often wondered if the city would ever appreciate the river, and we've seen how that appreciation has emerged in recent years. The new Phoenix Park created recreation opportunities, and the Confluence Project revitalized the river in downtown Eau Claire. Chippewa Falls has made plans to redesign the confluence with Duncan Creek and the Chippewa, making it more accessible to the community.

Apart from these civic undertakings, people all along the river can be found celebrating their waterway. In 2014, a "Celebrate the Lower Chippewa" event at Hobbs Ice Arena in Eau Claire featured prominent speakers on the environment. In 2015 Chippewa Falls celebrated the water with speakers, a band, and a dinner. The Ojibwe celebrate the river in their own way, by walking its shores. In a 2015 event that lasted five days, the Indigenous Peoples Task Force filled a bucket of water at New Post on LCO land and carried it 139 miles to the mouth of the river near Nelson.

During the ten years I paddled the Chippewa I worked as a corporate trainer, traveling by airplane, staying in fancy hotels—it was a fast life. Sometimes when I returned to the river, I was impatient. The canoe and the river seemed to hold me back, preventing me from the quicker pace I'd grown accustomed to. It forced me to slow down, and within a few hours I accepted the flow of the river and the limit of my paddle. I could be one with the river and the canoe.

I had a similar experience as I researched and wrote this book. Sometimes I had all of the river stories in my head at once, and the limits of the writing process seemed to hold everything back like a dam. I felt frustrated with the slowness of transferring my thoughts to paper and feared that my writing would disappoint the people who had entrusted their stories to me. All I could do was move forward, one word at a time, like putting the oar into the water again and again. As in my canoe, I set short-term goals—one section of river at a time. In the end, my fascination with the Chippewa and its stories propelled me forward.

With all that writing, all that paddling, behind me, you might think I've had my fill of the Chippewa. I spent years of my life immersed in this project. But the river flows on, ever constant and ever changing, so I will never truly be finished with it. I will find myself again and again on that bridge, watching and wondering what new stories are carried in the moving water.

Rivers are as timeless as poetry, exceeding geologic definitions. They flow past all of history and into the future.

Acknowledgments

I have been writing most of my life and would first like to ac-
knowledge those who encouraged me to share my writing with
others, starting with my friend Jim Martin, who suggested I send
an article on the Little Falls logging tragedy to a newspaper. Jerry
Poling helped my story to land on the front page of the *Eau Claire
Leader-Telegram* in time for the hundredth anniversary of the
drownings. Later I contacted Kathy Borkowski at the Wisconsin
Historical Society Press, who ended up guiding its publication in
the summer of 2006 edition of the *Wisconsin Magazine of History*.

As my interest in the Chippewa continued over several decades, many people helped and encouraged me. I was fortunate to
have the assistance of Adam Cahow, who believed in my ability to
turn this idea into a book and pointed me in the direction of *The
Wisconsin* by August Derleth, which became my model for this
project. I am thankful to the editors at the Wisconsin Historical
Society Press, including Kate Thompson, for seeing the potential
in my proposal, Erika Wittekind, who guided me in the editing
process, and Diane Drexler, who oversaw the production. Thank
you also to John Toren for his editing work.

Words cannot adequately express my appreciation and gratitude for the many, many people who shared their time and stories
with me as I made my way downriver. I have done my best to
capture their stories, and any imperfections are my responsibility. The residents of the Chippewa River Valley who welcomed
me into their communities and assisted me in my exploration

and research, roughly listed in the order I met them, were Pat Bonney, Larry Bay, Karen Powell, Ken Boness, Kathy Bay, Frank Kempf, Gregg Wangelin, Karen Thorp, Bernie Peterhansel, Cleon Schmidt, Roxanne Eder, Robert Petroski, Kacy Kempf, Sue Motola, Frank Motola, James R. Park, Michael Schwilk, John Dettloff, Brenda Dettloff, Gordon Thayer, Andrea Marple Wittwer, Barb Williamson, Janie Wise, Cheryl Treland, Harold Treland, Dr. Rick St. Germaine, Terrell Boettcher, Charlie Otto Rasmussen, Sean O'Connell, Denny Reyes, Neal Kephart, Kris Mayberry, Emmett A. Brown Jr., Chance Haldane, Moose Sporos, Tom Helsing, Dr. Penny Boileau, Sue Johnston, Jim Wilson, Blaire Shydlowski, Greg Haberman, Gary Gerber, David Frasch, Evie Frasch, Janet Gerber, Bimbo Gifford, Curt Gerber, Jim Gerber, Bob Villiard, Robert Sanders, Larry Sanders, Al Miller, Donnalene David, Richard LaBelle, Harold Flater, Tim Walters, Virginia Ellis, Bonnie Zinsli, Dick Zinsli, Lori Crabb, Joseph Baye, Steve Van Dam, Bryce O. Stenzel, Peter Wolfe, Lee Blanchard, Chuck Card, Marge Hebbring, Skip August, Dick Leinenkugel, Jason Smith, Gerald Jacobson, Les Davis, Don Birchner, Des Sikowski-Nelson, Rob Olson, Bill Nolte, Barb Powers, David Caradori, Patti Cigan, Nick Meyer, Jim Alf, Connie Ronnander, Renne Ponzio, Bob McCoy, Jack Kaiser, Dr. Doug Falkner, Dr. Sean Hartnett, Ray Larson, Dave Farr, John Benedict, S. Driever, Warren Barberg, Terry Mesch, Brian Gabriel, Bill Hogseth, Eleanor Wolf, Carl Morsbach, Mark Leach, David Linderud, and Bill Collins.

Several of my sources who have passed away since sharing their recollections with me deserve a special mention: Bill Cigan, Bernie Peterhansel, Phyllis DeBrot, Matt Hart, Jack O'Connell, and John "Little Bird" Anderson. I was fortunate to have the chance to know them and their stories.

I would also like to thank others who assisted me in my research, including Jerry Price, Norb Wurtzel, Matt Gundry, Tony Schuster, Brian Gabriel, Andrew Kennedy, Kristen Cornell

Gundry, and Logan Gundry. I also had the help of volunteers and employees at several organizations, museums, and libraries, including the Lower Chippewa River Alliance, Glidden Historical Society, Sawyer County Historical Society, Sherman and Ruth Weiss Community Library, Chippewa County Historical Society, Chippewa Valley Historical Society, L. E. Phillips Memorial Public Library, Pepin County Historical Society, Roseville Public Library, Durand Public Library, and the University of Wisconsin–Eau Claire Library.

And finally, I thank my children for accompanying me on various legs of this journey—their company and insights were invaluable—and my best friend and wife Dixie, who supported the cost and time invested in this project. She prefers a foggy day in London to a sunny one on the Chippewa, but she put up with all that was required to write this book.

Notes

Introduction

1. William Wordsworth, *The Prelude: The Four Texts (1798, 1799, 1805, 1850)* (London: Penguin, 2004), n.p.

Chapter 1

1. Robert H. Dott Jr. and John W. Attig, *Roadside Geology of Wisconsin* (Missoula, MT: Mountain Press Publishing Company, 2004), 23.

2. Ibid., 26.

3. Ibid., 24.

4. Ibid., 28.

5. Mark Wyman, *The Wisconsin Frontier* (Bloomington: Indiana University Press, 1998), 249.

6. Patty Loew, *Indian Nations of Wisconsin*, 2nd ed. (Madison: Wisconsin Historical Society Press, 2010), 60.

7. Tim Pfaff, *Paths of the People: The Ojibwe in the Chippewa Valley* (Eau Claire, WI: Chippewa Valley Museum Press, 1993), 10.

8. Ibid., 9.

9. William W. Warren, *History of the Ojibway People* (St. Paul: Minnesota Historical Society Press, 1984), 36.

10. Loew, *Indian Nations of Wisconsin*, 60.

11. Pfaff, *Paths of the People*, 11.

12. Rick St. Germaine, *A Brief History of Lac Courte Oreilles* (Duluth, MN: Holy Cow Press, 2012), 189–210.

13. Warren, *History of the Ojibway People*, 39.

14. Pfaff, *Paths of the People*, 11.

15. Wyman, *The Wisconsin Frontier*, 5–6.

16. Ibid., 38, 135.

17. Hamilton Nelson Ross, *La Point: Village Outpost on Madeline Island* (Madison: Wisconsin Historical Society Press, 2000), 20.

18. Arthur T. Adams, ed., *Explorations of Pierre Esprit Radisson* (Minneapolis: Ross Haines, 1961).

19. Ibid., 128.

20. Grace Lee Nute, *Caesars of the Wilderness* (St. Paul: Minnesota Historical Society Press, 1978).

21. Pfaff, *Paths of the People*, 11.

22. Paul H. Raihle, *The Valley Called Chippewa* (Cornell, WI: The Chippewa Valley Courier, 1940), 3.

23. Louis Hennepin, *Narrative of the Voyage to the Upper Mississippi* (Paris: 1683), 111.

24. Jonathan Carver, *The Journals of Jonathan Carver and Related Documents, 1766–1770*, ed. John Parker (St. Paul: Minnesota Historical Society Press, 1976), 5.

25. Ibid., 3.

26. John Vanek, "How the Chippewa River Got Its Name," *Currents*, newsletter of the Chippewa Valley Museum, Spring 2016, 15.

27. Jonathan Carver, *Carver's Travels in Wisconsin* (New York: Harper & Brothers, 1838), 89.

28. Ibid., 126–127.

29. Ibid., 166.

30. Chauncey H. Cooke, *Soldier Boy's Letters to His Father and Mother* (Independence, WI: Rainbow Press, 2004).

31. Mary Wingerd, *North Country: The Making of Minnesota* (Minneapolis: University of Minnesota Press, 2010), 212.

32. Ronald N. Satz, "Chippewa Treaty Rights: The Reserved Rights of Wisconsin's Chippewa Indians in Historical Perspective," *Transactions of the Wisconsin Academy of Sciences, Arts and Letters, vol. 79, no. 1* (Madison: Wisconsin Academy of Sciences, Arts, and Letters, 1991), 47.

33. Ibid., 55.

34. Ibid., 56.

35. Ibid.

36. Wyman, *The Wisconsin Frontier*, 223.

37. Satz, "Chippewa Treaty Rights," 57.

38. Wyman, *The Wisconsin Frontier*, 223.

39. Ibid., 225.

40. Satz, "Chippewa Treaty Rights," 66.

41. Richard E. Morse, "The Chippewas of Lake Superior," in *Wisconsin Historical Society Collections*, vol. 3 (Madison: Wisconsin Historical Society Press, 1904), 366.

Chapter 2

1. Henry Wadsworth Longfellow, *The Song of Hiawatha* (Jaffery, NH: David R. Godine Publishers, 2004), 81.

2. Thomas F. Water, *Wildstream: A Natural History of the Free Flowing River* (St. Paul, MN: Riparian Press, 2000), 75.

3. "Wisconsin Fur Trade," Milwaukee Public Museum, www.mpm.edu/research-collections/anthropology/online-collections-research/dubay-site/wisconsin-fur-trade.

4. Robert F. Fries, *Empire in Pine: The Story of Lumbering in Wisconsin, 1830–1900* (Ellison Bay, WI: Wm Caxton Ltd, 1989), 21.

5. William W. Bartlett, *History, Tradition and Adventure in the Chippewa Valley* (Chippewa Falls, WI: The Chippewa Printery, 1929), 183, www.cfla.us/Rambling/1929hocv.pdf.

6. Fries, *Empire in Pine*, 323.

7. Ibid., 207.

8. Malcolm Rosholt, *Lumbermen on the Chippewa* (Rosholt, WI: Rosholt House, 1982), 23.

9. Fries, *Empire in Pine*, 65.

10. Ibid., 22.

11. Walker D. Wyman, *The Lumberjack Frontier: Life of a Logger in the Early Days on the Chippeway* (Lincoln: University of Nebraska Press, 1969), 302.

12. Fries, *Empire in Pine*, 89.

13. George Perkins Marsh, *Man and Nature* (New York: Charles Scribner & Co, 1864), 3.

14. August Derleth, *The Wisconsin* (New York: Rinehart & Company, 1942), 182.

15. Wyman, *The Lumberjack Frontier*, 277.

16. Robert W. Wells, *Daylight in the Swamp* (Minocqua, WI: Northword Press, 1978), 181.

17. Fries, *Empire in Pine*, 238.

18. *History of the Glidden Four-Town Area* (Glidden, WI: Glidden Area Historical Society and Museum, 1984), 22.

19. Arlan Helgeson, *Farms in the Cutover Agricultural Settlement in Northern Wisconsin* (Madison: State Historical Society of Wisconsin, 1962).

20. Kenneth R. Boness, *Pile Driver: The Life of Charles "Midget" Fischer* (Bloomington, IN: Xlibris, 2002), 31.

21. Ibid., 44.

22. Ibid., 41.

23. Ibid., 48–52.

24. Ibid., 579.

25. Ibid., 727.

26. Ibid., 666.

27. Ibid., 697.

Chapter 3

1. Pat Bonney, interview with the author, January 9, 2009, Glidden, WI.

2. George P. Marsh, *Man and Nature; Or, Physical Geography as Modified by Human Action* (Cambridge, MA: Belknap Press of Harvard University Press, 1965).

3. The Glidden story is compiled from numerous conversations with Larry Bay, Pat Bonney, Karen Powell, and Frank Kempf, 2009–2010.

4. Dave Engel, *Shanagolden: An Industrial Romance* (Wisconsin Rapids, WI: River City Memoirs, 1990). Condensed from Engel's book with permission from the author.

5. Ibid., 44.

6. Ibid., 45.

7. Ibid.

Chapter 4

1. Jonathan Eig, *Get Capone* (New York: Simon and Schuster, 2011), 84, 89.

2. William W. Warren, *History of the Ojibway People* (St. Paul: Minnesota Historical Society Press, 1984), 191.

3. Charlie Otto Rasmussen, *Where the River Is Wide: Pahquahwong and the Chippewa Flowage* (Odahah, WI: Great Lakes Indian Fish and Wildlife Commission Press, 1998), 15.

4. "Wissota Hydro Generating Station," Xcel Energy, www.xcelenergy.com/ energy_portfolio/electricity/power_plants/wissota.

5. Rasmussen, *Where the River Is Wide,* 9, and Charlie Otto Rasmussen, interview with the author, November 4, 2011, Odanah, WI.

6. Ibid., 33.

7. Kathleen Tigerman, ed., *Wisconsin Indian Literature: Anthology of Native Voices* (Madison: University of Wisconsin Press, 2006), 105.

8. Thomas Vennum Jr., *Wild Rice and the Ojibway People* (St. Paul: Minnesota Historical Society Press, 1988), 39.

9. Denny Reyes, interview with the author, June 22, 2011, Hayward, WI.

10. Ralph W. Hidy, Frank Ernest Hill, and Allen Nevins, *Timber and Men: The Weyerhaeuser Story* (New York: The McMillian Company, 1963), 78.

11. August Derleth, *The Wisconsin* (New York: Rinehart and Company, 1942), 223–225.

12. Frances Densmore, *Chippewa Customs* (St. Paul: Minnesota Historical Society Press, 1979), 145.

13. John "Little Bird" Anderson, interview with the author, January 25, 2012, Springbrook, WI.

14. Todd Richmond, "Chippewa Leader Outlines Tribes' Grievances in Annual Speech," *St. Paul Pioneer Press*, April 10, 2013.

15. Gordon Thayer, interview with the author, February 11, 2012, Minneapolis, MN.

16. Andrea Marple Wittwer, interview with the author, January 25, 2012, Hayward, WI.

17. *Telemark Memories, 1947–1969* (Cable, WI: Telemark Educational Foundation, 2007).

18. Harold Treland, interview with the author, April 7, 2012, Hayward, WI.

19. Cheryl Treland, interview with the author, April 7, 2012, Hayward, WI.

20. Emmett Brown Jr., interview with the author, June 22, 2011, Hayward, WI.

21. Bill Linder-Scholer, interview with the author, June 26, 2011, WI, Namakagon, WI.

22. "Oral History Documentation: The Battle of the Horsefly," Chippewa Flowage Lake Association, www.cfla.us/History/horsefly.html.

23. John "Little Bird" Anderson, interview with the author, June 21, 2016, Springbrook, WI.

24. Brenda and John Dettloff and Phyllis DeBrot, interview with the author, October 12, 2011, Couderay, WI.

25. John O'Connell and Sean O'Connell, interview with the author, August 14, 2014, Eau Claire, WI.

Chapter 5

1. Sue Johnston, interview with the author, January 26, 2012, Winter, WI.

2. Jim Genrich, interview with the author, January 26, 2012, Winter, WI.

3. Dr. Penny Boileau, interview with the author, March 22, 2012, Winter, WI.

4. The John Dietz story is condensed from Malcolm Rosholt, *The Battle of Cameron Dam* (Rosholt, WI: Rosholt House, 1974).

5. Blaire Shydlowski, interview with the author, August 11, 2012, Winter, WI.

6. Jonathan Carver, *The Journals of Jonathan Carver and Related Documents, 1766–1770* (St. Paul: Minnesota Historical Society Press, 1976), 166.

7. Eldon Marple, "Frenchtown on the Chippewa," *Visitor*, June 15, 1979, 7.

8. *Canoe Trails of North Central Wisconsin* (Bruce, WI: North Central Canoe Trails Inc., 1977), 29.

Chapter 6

1. *Canoe Trails of North Central Wisconsin* (Bruce, WI: North Central Canoe Trails Inc., 1977), 30.

2. Ethel Elliot Chappell, *Around the Four Corners* (Rice Lake, WI: Chronotype, 1975), 210.

3. Harold Flater, interview with the author, August 28, 2015, Holcombe, WI.

4. James M. Campbell Sr., "Campbell: Chippewa River Flood Damage Exceeded $30,000 in '41," *The Chippewa Herald*, September 8, 2011, http://chippewa.com/lifestyles/article_cd991bde-da46-11e0-bf48-001cc4c03286.html.

5. "USGS 05360500 Flambeau River near Bruce, WI," US Geological Survey, http://waterdata.usgs.gov/nwis/uv?05360500.

6. Relative size of the Flambeau and Chippewa Rivers from Douglas Faulkner, associate professor, Department of Geology and Anthropology, University of Wisconsin–Eau Claire, e-mail correspondence with the author, December 30, 2014.

Chapter 7

1. Mark Wyman, *The Wisconsin Frontier* (Bloomington: Indiana University Press, 1998), 24.

2. Malcolm Rosholt, *Lumbermen on the Chippewa* (Rosholt, WI: Rosholt House, 1982), 147.

3. Ibid., 148.

4. Ibid., 151.

5. Ibid., 156.

6. The story of this tragedy is summarized from Richard Cornell, "Knights of the Spike-Soled Shoe," *Wisconsin Magazine of History* 89, no. 4 (2006): 38.

7. "Gives Review of Drowning," *Eau Claire Leader*, July 13, 1905.

8. "Holcombe Flowage," Wisconsin Department of Natural Resources, http://dnr.wi.gov/lakes/lakepages/lakedetail.aspx?wbic=2184900.

9. Tim Walters, interview with the author, March 31, 2015, Holcombe, WI.

10. "Brunet Island State Park," Wisconsin Department of Natural Resources, http://dnr.wi.gov/topic/parks/name/brunetisland/.

11. Darla Meyer, "Wilson Rawls Tells of Long Road to Success," *The Courier-Sentinel* (Cornell, WI), January 25, 1979, 10.

12. Diane Roback, "All-time Bestselling Children's Books," *Publisher's Weekly*, December 17, 2001, www.publishersweekly.com/pw/by-topic/childrens/childrens-industry-news/article/28595-all-time-bestselling-children-s-books.html.

13. Rosholt, *Lumbermen on the Chippewa*, 127.

14. William W. Bartlett, *History, Tradition and Adventure in the Chippewa Valley* (Chippewa Falls, WI: The Chippewa Printery, 1929), 183, www.cfla.us/Rambling/1929hocv.pdf.

15. Facts from Cornell's early life from Philip Dorf, *The Builder: A Biography of Ezra Cornell* (Ithaca, NY: The Dewitt Historical Society, 1952), 5–14. The Wisconsin pine story from Paul Wallace Gates, *The Wisconsin Pine Lands of Cornell University* (Madison: The State Historical Society of Wisconsin, 1943), 54, 59, 68, 92, 209, 241–243.

Chapter 8

1. J. A. Anderson, *A Life and Memoirs of Rev. C.F.X. Goldsmith* (Milwaukee: Evening Wisconsin Company, 1895). Digitized by Google, http://babel. hathitrust.org/cgi/pt?id=wu.89064865108;view=1up;seq=11.
2. Tom Giffey, "Festival Times Five: History of the Cadott Festivals," *Volume One*, July 8, 2015, 48.
3. Doug Faulkner, interview with the author, July 14, 2015, Eau Claire, WI.
4. The Jim Falls story of Old Abe is condensed from Richard Zeitlin, *Old Abe the War Eagle* (Madison: State Historical Society of Wisconsin, 1986).
5. "Lake Wissota State Park," Wisconsin Department of Natural Resources, http://dnr.wi.gov/topic/parks/name/lakewissota/.
6. Tony Schuster, interview with the author, August 17, 2015, Chippewa Falls, WI.
7. Rob Olson, interview with the author, August 24, 2015, Chippewa Falls, WI.

Chapter 9

1. "Irvine Park & Zoo," Chippewa Falls Chamber of Commerce, http://visitchippewafallswi.com/business/irvine-park-zoo.
2. Malcolm Rosholt, *Lumbermen on the Chippewa* (Rosholt, WI: Rosholt House, 1982), 112.
3. Chuck Card, telephone interview with the author, November 12, 2014.
4. J. A. Anderson, *A Life and Memoirs of Rev. C.F.X. Goldsmith* (Milwaukee: Evening Wisconsin Company, 1895), 45. Digitized by Google, http:// babel.hathitrust.org/cgi/pt?id=wu.89064865108;view=1up;seq=11.
5. Ibid., 65.
6. Ibid., 84.
7. Ibid., 106.
8. Ibid., 115.
9. Ibid.
10. Ibid., 145.
11. Marge Hebbring, interview with the author, April 14, 2015, Chippewa Falls, WI.
12. Donna Bourget, interview with the author, April 14, 2015, Chippewa Falls, WI.
13. Jason Smith, interview with the author, November 12, 2014, Chippewa Falls, WI.
14. "Cray Research at Chippewa Falls: A Story of the Supercomputer," Chippewa Falls Museum of Industry and Technology, YouTube video, 48:09, posted by ThisMakesMeThink, January 7, 2014, www.youtube.com/ watch?v=wn03wn3k47Y.

15. Rod Pike, telephone interview with the author, April 15, 2015.

16. "History: Cray's Rich History Extends Back to 1972," Cray, www.cray. com./company/history.

17. Pike, interview.

18. Les Davis, telephone interview with the author, August 1, 2016.

19. Noel Stock, *The Life of Ezra Pound* (New York: Routledge, 1970) 150.

20. *Chippewa Valley, Wisconsin: Past and Present* (Chicago: S. J. Clarke, 1913). Full text available at https://archive.org/stream/chippe-wacountywi11unse/chippewacountywi11unse_djvu.txt.

21. The Chippewa Springs story is condensed from the 100th Anniversary Special Collectors Edition of *Chippewa Spring Water* (Chippewa Falls, WI: Herald Telegram, 1993). Thanks to Adam Cahow for sharing this.

22. Jeff Engel, "Miller Brewing Acquisition Helped Leinenkugel's Reach Six Generations," *Milwaukee Business Journal*, September. 28, 2013, www. bizjournals.com/milwaukee/blog/2013/09/miller-acquisition-helped. html.

23. Ibid.

24. Dick Leinenkugel, interview with the author, August 17, 2015, Chippewa Falls, WI.

25. Dave Gordon, interview with the author, April 22, 2015, Chippewa Falls, WI.

26. "Cray Research at Chippewa Falls," video.

Chapter 10

1. "Dells Pond," Wisconsin Department of Natural Resources, http://dnr. wi.gov/lakes/lakepages/lakeDetail.aspx?wbic=2149900.

2. "Half Moon Lake," University of Wisconsin–Eau Claire Department of Geography and Anthropology, http://people.uwec.edu/jolhm/ Halfmoon/Sawmills%20.htm.

3. Dale Arthur Peterson, "Lumbering on the Chippewa in the Eau Claire Area, 1845–1885" (PhD diss., University of Minnesota, 1970), 513.

4. Ibid., 526.

5. "The Log Flume," Wisconsin Historical Markers website, http:// wisconsinhistoricalmarkers.blogspot.com/2014/07/the-log-flume-dells-pond-to-half-moon.html.

6. Bill Gharrity, "Flume Doom," *Eau Claire Leader Telegram*, August 9, 1990.

7. "Dells Hydro Generating Station," Xcel Energy, www.xcelenergy.com/ energy_portfolio/electricity/power_plants/dells.

8. "Carson Park History," Chippewa Valley Museum, www.cvmuseum.com/ when_you_get_here/sub06a_carson_park_history.phtml.

9. "1952 Eau Claire Bears," Baseball-Reference.com, www.baseball-reference. com/register/team.cgi?id=b3039f33.

10. "Hank Aaron Biography," ESPN, www.espn.com/mlb/player/bio/_/ id/17499/hank-aaron.

11. "Hank Aaron Biography," Biography.com, www.biography.com/people/ hank-aaron-9173497#legacy.

12. Jerry Poling, *A Summer Up North* (Madison: University of Wisconsin Press, 2002), xv–xvi.

13. Ibid., 66.

14. Ibid., 15.

15. Ibid., 81.

16. Glenn St. Arnault, *Play Ball: The Saint's 55 Years in Eau Claire Baseball* (Eau Claire, WI: St. Arnault, 2013), 86.

17. Luc Anthony, "Expressing Success," *Volume One,* June 10, 2015, 65.

18. "Health Care," Eau Claire Area Economic Development Corporation, www.eauclaire-wi.com/resources/health-care.

19. Conversation with Ray Larson, Dave Farr, John Benedict, S. Driever, and Warren Barberg at the Grand Avenue Café, June 4, 2015.

20. "News: Fournier's for a Night," Chippewa Valley Museum, August 5, 2014, www.cvmuseum.com/news.phtml/776422C8/ fourniers_for_a_night/.

21. Larry Lehmer, *The Day the Music Died* (New York: Shermer Trade Books, 1997), 70–71.

22. Bill Nolte, interview with the author, September 4, 2014, Eau Claire, WI.

23. Jon Caramanica, "Who, What and Where Is Bon Iver?" *New York Times,* June 3, 2011.

24. Nick Meyer, interview with the author, September 4, 2014, Eau Claire, WI.

25. Ibid.

26. Tom Giffey, "Festival Times Five: History of the Cadott Festivals," *Volume One,* July 8, 2015, 50.

27. Doris Arnold, *Remembering Eau Claire* (Eau Claire, WI: Arnold, 1960), 11–12.

28. Joseph O. Barrett, *The Soldier Bird, "Old Abe": The Live War Eagle of Wisconsin, that Served a Three Years' Campaign in the Great Rebellion,* 3rd ed. (Madison, WI: Atwood & Culver Publishers, 1876), 51.

29. Jonathan Carver, *The Journals of Jonathan Carver and Related Documents, 1766–1770* ed. John Parker (St. Paul: Minnesota Historical Society Press, 1976), 163.

30. "Campus History," University of Wisconsin–Eau Claire, www.uwec.edu/about/campus-history/.

31. "Council Oak Display," University of Wisconsin–Eau Claire, November 5, 2013, www.uwec.edu/centers/facilities/art/council.htm.

32. Jerry Jacobson, interview with the author, April 18, 2013, Chippewa Falls, WI.

33. *CVTC: A Century of Proven Education* (Eau Claire, WI: Chippewa Valley Technical College, 2012), 47.

34. Malcolm Rosholt, *Lumbermen on the Chippewa* (Rosholt, WI: Rosholt House, 1982), 129.

35. *Business Atlas of the City of Eau Claire, 1888* (Eau Claire, WI: L.E. Phillips Library, 1888), 11.

36. Matt and Susan Tietz, interview with the author, April 22, 2015, Eau Claire, WI.

37. "Uniroyal Inc. Records, 1917–1990," L. E. Phillips Public Library, Eau Claire, WI.

38. *Business 2010 Hall of Fame Inductees* (Eau Claire, WI: Eau Claire Area Chamber of Commerce, 2010), 5.

39. Ibid.

40. Bob McCoy, interview with the author, July 9, 2015, Eau Claire, WI.

41. Jack Kaiser, telephone interview with the author, July 15, 2015.

Chapter 11

1. Douglas Faulkner, email message to the author, January 27, 2015.

2. David Caradori, interview with the author, June 4, 2015, Eau Claire, WI.

3. Facts of the Silver Mine Hill story condensed from the *129th Annual Silver Mine Hill* (Eau Claire, WI: Eau Claire Ski Club, 2015).

4. "Chippewa River State Trail," Wisconsin Department of Natural Resources, http://dnr.wi.gov/topic/parks/name/chiprivertrail/.

5. Jim Alf, *When the Ferries Still Ran* (Eau Claire: Eau Claire Printing Company, 2006), 27.

6. Jim Alf, interview with the author, July 13, 2016, Eau Claire, WI.

7. Phil Dinges, "The Truth Behind the Caryville Myths," WEAU 13 News, October 31, 2007, www.weau.com/home/headlines/10930481.html.

8. Brian Gabriel, interview with the author, September 4, 2015, Meridean, WI. Many videos filmed on the Lower Chippewa can be viewed on Gabriel's Facebook page, The Chippewa Bottoms Journey: www.facebook.com/chippewa.journey.

9. Mark Twain, *Life on the Mississippi* (New York: Harper & Brothers, 1902), 30–31.

10. Laura Ingalls Wilder, *Little House on the Prairie* (New York: Harper Collins, 1925), 8.

11. Kathryn R. Goetz, "The Story Behind the Stories: Laura Ingalls Wilder's Life in Minnesota and Beyond," MinnPost, August 19, 2014.

12. Elizabeth Clarke Hardy, "Durand," School District of Durand, http://
web.durand.k12.wi.us/hs/history/ECHardy/page2.htm.

13. "A Letter from Alonzo (Lon Maxwell) Williams to Elder Downer of Arkansaw," School District of Durand, http://web.durand.k12.wi.us/hs/
history/WilliamsToDowner/WilliamsToDowner.htm.

14. John E. Hallwas, *Dime Novel Desperadoes: The Notorious Maxwell
Brothers* (Champaign: University of Illinois Press, 2011), 235–236.

15. Thanks to Terry Mesch for the story. Coverage in the following: "Max-
well in Manacles," *St. Paul Pioneer Press*, November 18, 1881, quoted in
Hallwas, *Dime Novel Desperadoes*, 222; Untitled article, *Pepin County
Courier*, November 18, 1881, quoted in Hallwas, *Dime Novel Despera-
does*, 209; "Positive He Arrested Ed Maxwell," Pepin County Courier,
November 15, 1881; Buz Swerkstrom, "Durand Mob Made History,"
Eau Claire Leader Telegram, November 13, 1981; Les Kruger, Broth-
ers in Blood (Tucson, AZ: Wheatmark, 2008); Hallwas, *Dime Novel
Desperadoes*.

16. "Helen Parkhurst," Little Dalton, www.littledalton.com/helen-parkhurst.

17. Mark Wyman, *The Wisconsin Frontier* (Bloomington: Indiana University
Press, 1998), 268.

18. Malcolm Rosholt, *Lumbermen on the Chippewa* (Rosholt, WI: Rosholt
House, 1982), 233.

19. Ibid., 235.

20. Chauncey H. Cooke, *Soldier Boy's Letters to His Father and Mother,
1861–5* (Independence, WI: Rainbow Press, 2004), 135.

21. Rick St. Germaine, *A Brief History of Lac Courte Oreilles* (Duluth, MN:
Holy Cow Press, 2012); and William W. Bartlett, *History, Tradition and
Adventure in the Chippewa Valley* (Chippewa Falls, WI: Chippewa
Printery, 1929), www.cfla.us/Rambling/1929hocv.pdf.

22. William W. Warren, *History of the Ojibway People* (St. Paul: Minnesota
Historical Society Press, 1984), 305–307.

23. "Corporate Responsibility Report: Tyrone Property Restoration," Xcel
Energy, www.xcelenergy.com/staticfiles/xe/Corporate/CRR2012/envi-
ronment/biodiversity/tyrone-property.html.

24. Joe Knight, "Knight Life: Land Purchase Will Ensure Land Where Nu-
clear Plant Was Once Proposed Will Remain Natural," *Eau Claire Leader
Telegram*, August 6, 2016, www.leadertelegram.com/News/Front-
Page/2016/08/05/Preserving-nature.html.

25. Robert H. Dott and John W. Attig, *Roadside Geology of Wisconsin*
(Missoula, MT: Mountain Press Publishing, 2004), 176–178.

26. John Anfinson, *The River We Have Wrought: A History of the Upper Mississippi* (Minneapolis: University of Minnesota Press, 2003), 282.

Index

Note: Page numbers in *italics* refer to illustrations.

Aaron, Hank, 168–169, *169*, 204
Ackroyd, Peter, 2
Alf, Jim, 187
Allen Park (Chippewa Falls, WI), 159
American Birkebeiner, 71–72
American Indian Movement (AIM), 59
American Indians, treaties, 15–20, 26, 41, 57, 78
Amoco Foam Products plant, 160
Ancient Order of Hiberians, 157
Anderson, Dave, 80
Anderson, J. A., 156
Anderson, John "Little Bird," 61–65, *63*, 82
Aney, Dennis, 33, 54–55
Anishinaabe, 8–9. *See also* Odawa; Ojibwe
Anson Park (Jim Falls, WI), 141
April Base, 173
Armstrong, Benjamin, 17–19
Armstrong, Louis, 172
Arnold, Doris, 175
Arpin Dam, 93, 103
arts centers, 155, 181
Ashland (WI), 11, *12*
Ashland County (WI), 20, 168–169
Atkinson, Rick, 4
August, Skip, 164

Bacon, James "Beef Slough," 195
Bad River Reservation, 19, 61
Balbin, Sara, 62–64
Banbury (business incubator), 181
Banks, Dennis, 204
Barber Lake, 87
Barker Lake, 55
Barrett, Joseph O., 175
Bartlett, William, 26, 130
baseball, 168–170
Battle of Cameron Dam, 101
Bay Road Bridge, 33
Bear Lake, 34, 36, 46, 109
Beef Slough Company, 195

Belille, Charles, 86, 106
Belille Falls, 92, 157
Bellegarde, France, 92
Bieze, Laurie, 184–185
Big Bend (Chippewa River), 112, 114
Big Mill (Chippewa Falls, WI), 151, 153–154, 159
Big Ojibway (Ojibwe war chief), 196–197
bike trails, 2, 125, 186, 205
Billy Boy Dam, 105
Biography of the Thames (Ackroyd), 2
birchbark canoes, 10, 23, 106, 157
Bishops Bridge, 94, 97, 184
Black Bear Capital of Wisconsin (Glidden), 25
Black Bear Forest Products, 41
black bears, 25, 45–46
Black School (Arkansaw, WI), 194
Blaisdell Lake, 53, 55
Blanchard, Lee, 126, *127*, 130, 143–144
Blanchard, Louie, 27–28, 126, 143
Blue Hills, 112
Bob Creek, 126
Boettcher, Terrell, 68, 75
Boggie's Bar, 114–115
Boileau, Penny, 86–88
Bon Iver (band), 173
"Bonaparte's Retreat" (fiddle tune), 144
Boness, Ken, 36
Bonney, Pat, 5–6, 32, 39–40, 47–50, *49*, 51, 205
Bourget, Donna, 158–159
Bow and Arrow Resort, 65
Brackett, Saul, 122, *123*, 171
Bradley, Larry, 141
Brown, Emmett, Jr., 76–77, 78
Bruce (WI), 95, 108–117
Bruin Restaurant (Glidden, WI), 25, 45–46, 47
Brunet, Jean, 26, 125, 129, *131*, *159*
Brunet Falls, 134, 157
Brunet Island State Park, 125
Brunet River, 93, 98
Brush Island, 187
Buddyrevelles (band), 174

Buffalo, Chief, 17–20, *18*, *19*
buffalo, in Chippewa Valley, 13–14
Butternut (WI), 34–35, 36, 42

Cadott, Village of (WI), 141, 158–159, 174
Cadotte, Michel, 146, 151, 152, 158
Caesars of the Wilderness (Nute), 11–12
Cahow, Adam, 3–4, 70, 93, 115, 123, 203
Cameron, Hugh, 98
Cameron Dam, Battle of, 101
Camp McCain (near Greenwood, MS), 92
camping and campsites, 37, 53, 55, 91,
    125, 150
Canadian National Railway, 111
canoe races, 94–95, 97
canoes and canoeing. *See also* rapids; *and
    names of specific canoers*: author and
    family canoes, 22, 23, 89, 108, 119,
    136; birchbark canoes, 10, 23, 106, 157;
    wind problems, 53–54, 92, 119–120,
    147–149
Capone, Al, 80
Caradori, David, 184, *185*
Card, Chuck, 151, 154–155, *154*, 157
Carson Park (Eau Claire, WI), 168–170
Cartier, Jacques, 11
Carver, Jonathan, 13–14, 56, 104, 105, 177
Caryville (WI), 187
Central Amateur Athletic Union
    championship (wrestling), 35
Champlain, Samuel de, 11
Chariots of Fire (movie), 36
Chequamegon National Forest, 28, 41, 44
Chicago (IL), 35, 50
Chief River, 85
Chippewa County Historical Society, 146,
    152, 155, *158*, 164
Chippewa County, Wisconsin (book),
    162–163
Chippewa Crossing (now Glidden, WI),
    30, 46
Chippewa Dam, 145, *146*, 148
Chippewa Falls (falls), 157
Chippewa Falls (WI), *152*; sawmills, 27,
    130; stories and people, 106, 151–164
Chippewa Flowage (lake), 19, 53–83, 85,
    94–97, 202
Chippewa Lake (Bayfield County, WI),
    6–7, 31, 77

Chippewa Lumber and Boom (CLB),
    98–100, 123, 126, 130, 151–152,
    153–154, 155
Chippewa River: confluence with Flambeau
    River, *116*, 117; East Fork, 5–7, 7,
    21–25, 53; history summarized, 202–
    207; Lower Chippewa, 141, 183–201;
    names for, 9, 13; origins of, 5–20;
    regulating water flow, 94–97; sand and,
    183–184, 199–200; watershed, *viii*, 70;
    West Fork, 6–7, 31, 77–78, 85; wild
    Chippewa, 118–137, *148*, 203
Chippewa River bike trail, 186
Chippewa River Rendezvous, 127
Chippewa Spring Water, 162
Chippewa Springs, 162–163
Chippewa Trail, 56, 86
Chippewa Valley Motor Car train, 197
Chippewa Valley Museum (Eau Claire,
    WI), 171
Chippewa Valley Technical College
    (CVTC), 178
Chippewa Village (former town), 72, 146
Christmas Village (Chippewa Falls, WI), 152
Church Island, 79
Cigan, Bill, 180–181, *180*
Cigan, Patti, *180*, 181
Civilian Conservation Corps camp, 37
Clam Lake, 7, 31, 77
Clemens, Samuel, 186, 189. *See also* Twain,
    Mark
Cloquet (MN), 41
Colbert River, 13. *See also* Mississippi River
Coleman, Charles and Milton, 192–193
Confluence Project (Eau Claire, WI), 181
Cooke, C. H., 14, 195
Cornell (WI), 26, 27, 119, 125, 126, 132
Cornell, Brian (author's son), 89–93, *90*,
    119–120, 134–136
Cornell, Dixie (author's wife), 110, 120,
    190, 200, 205–206
Cornell, Ezra, 41, 130–132
Cornell, Kari (author's daughter-in-law),
    119–120, 134–136
Cornell, KC (author's daughter): East Fork
    trips, 21–25, 31–34, 36–38, 53–55;
    Eau Claire trip, 176; Highway 8 to
    Flater's Resort, 112–117; Highway D
    to Highway 8, 108–110; Holcombe

Dam to Cornell, 124–125; Jim Falls to Lake Wissota, 138–140, 142, 145–150; Lower Chippewa trips, 184, 187, 196, 200–201; photos, *22, 54, 90, 135*; trip to Jim Falls, 134–136; West Fork source, 31; wild Chippewa trip, 119–120; Winter Dam to Highway D, 89–93

Cornell, Kristen. *See* Cornell, KC (author's daughter)

Cornell, Richard D.: Eau Claire trip, 176–182; Highway 8 to Flater's Resort, 112–117; Highway D to Highway 8, 108–110; Holcombe Dam to Cornell, 124–125; Jim Falls to Lake Wissota, 138–140, 142, 145–150; Lower Chippewa trips, 184, 187, 196, 200–201; memories of father, 92; photos, *90, 104, 135*; and river stories, 204–207; trip to Jim Falls, 134–136; Winter Dam to Highway D, 89–93

Cornell, W. J., 130

Cornell Courier Sentinel (newspaper), 126, 128

Cornell Dam, 95, 125, 129, 134, 203

Cornell University (Ithaca, NY), 41, 132

Couderay River, 12, 13, 14, 103–106

Council Oak (Eau Claire, WI), 178

Country Fest (Cadott, WI), 141, 174

Country Jam (Eau Claire, WI), 175

Crabb, Dylan, *132*, 133–134

Crabb, Lori, *133*, 134

Craker, Kari, 133

cranberries, 44, 58, 80

Cray, Seymour, Jr., 160, 161

Cray, Seymour, Sr., 161

Cray Research, 161–162, 178

dairy herd, 133–134

Dakota, and Ojibwe, 10, 15, 78, 178, 196–197

Dalton School, 194–195

dams and dam building. *See also individual dam names*: consequences of, 60–61, 150; in Eau Claire area, 167; lake creation, 123; Little Falls dam tragedy (1905), 118, *119*, 120–123, 171; relicensing process, 61, 113, 203–204; and river history, 118

David, Donnalene, 111

Day Lake Recreation Area, 77

DeBrot, Billy, 55, 72

DeBrot, Phyllis, 74, 75, 78–79

Dells Dam (1878), 57, 167–168.

Dells Dam (1924), 165, 168

Dells Pond (Eau Claire, WI), 165

Derleth, August, 2, 28–29

Des Groseilliers, Medart Chouart, 11–12, 105

Dettloff, John and Brenda, 74, 75–76, 78–79, 82

Dietz, John, 97–101, *99*

Dix's Chalet (Winter, WI), 91

DNR. *See* Wisconsin DNR (Department of Natural Resources)

Dressel, John, 122

drug recovery program graduation, 64–65

Druschke, Dick, 49

duck race fund-raiser, 88–89, 94, 101, 102

Duncan Creek, 157, 159, 160

Durand (WI), 166, 183, 184, 186, 189–196

Dylan's Dairy, 133–134, *133*

eagle sightings, 78, 90–91, 109

Eagle Valley Raceway, 136–137

East Fork, Chippewa River, 5–7, *7*, 21–25, 53

East Fork Resort, 55

Eau Claire Badgers (militia company), 144, 175–176

Eau Claire Cavaliers (baseball team), 168, 169–170

Eau Claire Dam, 95

Eau Claire Express (baseball team), 170

Eau Claire High School, 171

Eau Claire Landmarks Commission, 172

Eau Claire River, 28, 179

Eau Claire (WI), 165, *166*; relationship with Chippewa River, 205–206; sawmills in, 27, 166–167; stories and people, 165–182

Eighth Wisconsin Infantry Regiment, 127, 144–145, *144*

ELF (extremely low frequency) system, 32, 33

elk herd, 40, 77–78

Ella (WI), 196, 198–199

Ellington, Mercer, 172

Ellis, Virginia, 127, 128

Engel, Dave, 44

England, Billy "the Beaver," 120

environmental protections, history of, 28, 59–62, 67, 96, 150
Exeland (WI), 94, 107

Falbe, Beverly, 126
Famous Dave's restaurant chain, 80
Faulkner, Doug, 141, 166–167
Favre, Brett, 103
Federal Energy Regulatory Commission, 61
ferry crossings, 113, 187
Fillmore, Millard, 17–19
fires, 44, 153
First Nations Recovery Center, 65
Fischer, Charlie, 34–36, *35*, 46
fishing and fishermen: 1920s boom, 31; Bimbo Gifford equipment, 103; musky fishing, 34, 55–56, 75–77; near Winter Dam, 90; resorts for, 55–56, 72–73, 75–76; sturgeon fishing, 141; walleye fishing, 34, 75–76
Fishing Without Borders, 76
Five-Mile Bluff, 199
Flambeau Ridge, 112, 114
Flambeau River, 28, 100, *116*, 117, 143
Flambeau River Papers Mill (Park Falls, WI), 42
Flater, Harold, 115–116
Flater, Linda, 133
Flater's Resort, 112–117, *118*
floods, 115, 120, 139, 187, 204–205
Flying Eagles (ski club), 185
Fournier, Wenceslas, 171
Fournier's Ballroom, 171–172
frac sand trains, 110–111
Frasch, David, 77–78
French Canadians, 26, 56, 79
French immigrants. *See* Brunet, Jean; Fournier, Wenceslas
fur trade, 11, 12, 15–16, 25–26, 56, 157–159
Fur Trade Days (Chippewa Falls, WI), 164

Gabriel, Brian, 188–189, *188*
Gagnon, Andrew, 122
Galloway Street (Eau Claire, WI), 179
Gauthier, Francis, 130
Genrich, James, 87, 88
Gerber, Janet, 102
German immigrants, 26, 30, 42, 195, 199

Giffey, Tom, 174–175
Gifford, Bimbo, 102–104, 106–107
Gillette Safety Tire Company, 179
glaciers and glacial melting, 7–8, 70, 77, 112, 147
Glen Loch Dam, 153
Glidden (WI), 5; Fourth of July and Labor Day celebrations, 50–51; and lumber industry, 25, 30–31, 41–42; stories and people, 39–52
Glidden Enterprise (newspaper), 5, 31, 32, 39–40, 45–46, 47–50
Glidden High School, 51
Glidden History Museum, 25, 51
Goldsmith, Charles, 139, 151, 155–157
Goldstar Tech (business), 181
Goose Eye rapids, 55
Gordon, Dave, 164
Grand Avenue Café (Eau Claire, WI), 171
Grand Rapids (now Wisconsin Rapids, WI), 42–44
Great Walls of Glidden, 47, *48*
Gregg's Steak House (later the Glidd Inn), 45
Groseilliers, Medart Chouart des. *See* Des Groseilliers, Medart Chouart
Gundry, Kristen. *See* Cornell, KC (author's daughter)
Gundry, Matt (author's son-in-law), 176, 196

Haberman, Greg, 94, *95*, 96–97
Half Moon Lake, 166, 167
Hall, S. A., 14
Hallie (WI), 160, 161
Hamline University (St. Paul, MN), 24
Hannibal, Missouri, 189
Happy Island, 187
Hardy, Elizabeth Clarke, 191–192
Harms, Cecilia, 128
Hart, Robert and Matt, 31–33, 47
Hartnett, Sean, 203
Harvest of Friends Food Pantry, 86, 89, *100*, 101–102
Hayward (WI), 68, 70–72, 73, 76–77
Hayward School Journal, 106
health care centers, 171
Hebbring, Marge, 146, 151–152, 157, *158*
Helsing, Tom, 97
Helsing's bar, 97, *104*, 105
Hennepin, Louis, 13

Heyde Center for the Arts (Chippewa Falls, WI), 155
Hiawatha's Sailing (Longfellow), 23
historical markers, 97–98, 105, 129, 136, 140, 167
Historyland (Hayward, WI), 72
Hogseth, Mike, 197
Holcombe (WI), 121
Holcombe Dam, 95, 115, 124
Holcombe Flowage (lake), 60, 123–124
Holly, Buddy, 172
Honor Shoppe, 180
Honor the Earth Powwow, 79–80, 81
Horne, Ole "Whitewater," 122–123
Hospital Sisters of St. Francis, 157
House in the Woods, 43, 44
Hunter Lake, 55
Husse, Fannie, 192
hydroelectric power, 56–61, 168, 203–204. See also Northern States Power (NSP); Xcel Energy

Ice Age Trail, 125, 150
Ida Campbell (boat), 166
immigrants: education for, 178; French immigrants (see Brunet, Jean; Fournier, Wenceslas); German immigrants, 26, 30, 42, 195, 199; Irish immigrants, 27; and lumber industry, 26–27, 29–30; Norwegian immigrants, 26, 72, 73; Polish immigrants, 26; and promotion of Glidden, 30–31
Indian Removal Act (1830), 16
Indian Trail Resort, 74, 75–76, 78–79, 84–85
Irish immigrants, 27
Irvine, William, 98, 130, 153–154, 153
Irvine Park (Chippewa Falls, WI), 152, 153
Itasca, Lake, 24

Jackson Milling Company (Stevens Point, WI), 44
Jacobs, Town of (WI), 46
Jacobson, Jerry, 178
Jamal, Ahmad, 172
Jeffers, S. M., 175
Jim Falls dam, 95, 136, 138–139
Jim Falls (WI), 138–147
Johnson, Dean, 103
Johnston, Sue, 86–87

Joynt, the (Eau Claire, WI), 172–173
Jump River, 28

Kaiser, Jack, 181
Karls, Dale, 174
Kempf, Frank, 51
Kennedy, Andrew (author's son): visit to Couderay River source, 104, 105; visit to Glidden area, 3, 38–40, 45–47; wild Chippewa trip, 119–120
Kephart, Neal, 82
Killian, Joseph, 193
"King of the Chippewa River" carving, 121, 121
Knight, Miletus, 192

La Follette, Robert M., 60
La Pointe County, 20
La Pointe (WI), 11, 20, 106
LaBelle, Richard, 110–111
Lac Courte Oreilles Education Advancement Resource Network (LEARN), 64
Lac Courte Oreilles Journal, 59
Lac Courte Oreilles (lake), 11, 104
Lac Courte Oreilles (LCO) Ojibwe: casino, 70, 80, 84; Honor the Earth Powwow, 79–80, 81; Tribal Council, 65–68; and Winter Dam, 56–60
Lac Courte Oreilles Ojibwa Community College, 64, 104
Lac Courte Oreilles Reservation, 19–20, 56
Lac Coutereille, 9
Lac du Flambeau Reservation, 19
Lake Wissota State Park, 150
lakes. See individual lake names
Lakewood Café (Winter, WI), 92
Land-Grant College Act, 41, 131
Landing Resort, 59, 85
Laurentide Ice Sheet, 7–8
LCO. See Lac Courte Oreilles (LCO) Ojibwe
LCO Casino, Lodge and Convention Center, 70, 80, 84
LEARN Commission, 64
"Legend of the Chippewa Spring and Minnehaha, the Indian Maiden" (Pound), 162–163
Leinenkugel, Dick, 151–152, 163–164

Leinenkugel, Jacob, 156, 163
Leinenkugel beer and brewery, 153, 161, 163–164
Life on the Mississippi (Twain), 2, 189
Linder-Scholer, Bill, 77
Little Falls dam, 118, *119*, 120–123, 171
Little Falls (falls), 157
Little House in the Big Woods (Wilder), 191
Little Lac Courte Oreilles (lake), 104
Little Niagara Creek, 176, *177*
Local Store (Eau Claire, WI), 174, 179
logging and loggers. *See* lumber industry
Long, Brian, 46
Longfellow, Henry Wadsworth, 23
Lower Chippewa, 141, 183–201
Lower Chippewa River Alliance, 183, 198
lumber industry: in Chippewa River Valley, 8, 25–31, 41; Dietz conflict, 97–101; Eau Claire area, 165–168; and hardwoods, 30, 124; Little Falls dam tragedy (1905), 121–123; Paul Bunyan Logging Camp Museum, 170–171; present-day methods, 123–124; and railroads, 28, 30, 106–107; worker nationalities, 26–27; World Lumberjack Championship, 71
The Lumberjack Frontier (Wyman), 126, 143
Luther Hospital, 171
lynching incident (Durand, WI), 192–194
Lyons, Luke, 121

MacArthur Hotel (Bruce, WI), 111, *112*
Madeline Island, 9, 10, 20
Make-A-Wish Foundation, 133
Mallard's Resort, 149
manoomin, 58
map, Chippewa Watershed, *viii*
Marder, John, 126
Marion Park (Glidden, WI), 49–51
Marple, Eldon, *69*, 70, 106
Marsh, George Perkins, 28
Maslowski Park (Ashland, WI), 11, 12
Mason Shoe Outlet Store (Chippewa Falls, WI), 152
Maxwell, Ed and Lon, 192–194
Mayberry, Kris, 82
mayflies, 37
Mayo Clinic Health System, 171
McCann, Dan, 136, 143–144

McClain, David, 145
McCoy, Bob, 181
McDonell Memorial High School, 155
McDonough (manufacturing company), 179
McNamer, Diane, 71
Medill, William, 16
Mellon Lumber Company, 44
Memorial High School (Eau Claire, WI), 24, 145
Meredith, Kelley, 47
Meridean (WI), 187–188
Merk, Frederick, 29
Mesch, Terry, *190*
Meyer, Nick, 174, 181
"Midgets" (Butternut School District team name), 36
Mille Lacs, Lake, 13
Miller, Al, 110–111
Milwaukee Braves (baseball team), 168
mining industry, 61–62
"Mission Possible" slogan, 67, 80
Mississippi River, 2–3, 11, 13, 23–24, 184, 189, 200. *See also* Pepin, Lake
Mississippi River Logging Company (MRL Co.), 179, 195
Moe, Kathy, 82
Mole Lake Reservation, 19
Monitor (boat), 156
Montessori, Maria, 194
Moose Lake, 78
Morrill Act, 41, 131
Morsbach, Carl, 198–199
Most Precious Blood Catholic Church (Glidden, WI), 25
Mount Simon Park (Eau Claire, WI), 165
murals (Glidden, WI), 46, 47, *48*
Musavage, Joe and Rose, 54
music festivals, 141, 174–175, 186
Musky Fest (Hayward, WI), 76, 77
musky fishing, 34, 55–56, 75–77

Nanabozho, 58
Narrative of the Voyage to the Upper Mississippi (Hennepin), 13
Nash, Guy, 42–45
Nash, Jim, 42–43
Nash, Tom, 42
Nash Lumber Company (Shanagolden, WI), 43–44

National Fresh Water Fishing Hall of Fame, 76
National Register of Historic Places, 155
Nekoosa Lumber Mill (Grand Rapids, WI),
    42
Nenaangebi, 196
New Meridean (WI), 189
New York Times, 173–174, 194
Nicolet National Forest, 28
Nolte, Bill, 172–173, *173*
Norte Antiques, 110
Northern States Power (NSP), 58, 59, 79,
    125, 161. *See also* Xcel Energy
Northern Wisconsin Elk Reintroduction
    Project, 77–78
Northern Wisconsin State Fair, 164
Northwestern Lumberman, 29
Norwegian immigrants, 26, 72, 73
Notre Dame, Church of (Chippewa Falls,
    WI), 155, 156, 157
Nute, Grace, 11–12

Oak Shores, 75
O'Connell, Jack and Sean, 82–83
Odawa, 9, 10, 12, 56, 105
Odawasagaegun, 9, 12
Odetta (folk singer), 172–173
Office of the Commissioner of Railroads, 111
Ojibwa Community Club canoe race,
    94–95, 97
Ojibwa Park, 89–92
Ojibwe: and Dakota, 10, 15, 78, 178,
    196–197; delegation to Washington
    (1853), *19*; fur trade and, 15–16;
    history, 56–60, 104–105; name origins,
    9; relationship with Chippewa River,
    206; reservations, creation of, 19–20;
    treaties, 15–20, 26, 41, 57, 78
Old Abe bike trail, 125
Old Abe (eagle), 142–145, *144*, 175–176
Old Abe marker (Highway 178), 136
Old Abe sculpture (Jim Falls, WI), 140, *143*
Olson, Rob, 150
Olympic Games (Paris, France, 1924),
    35–36
O'Neil Creek, 149
Orange Bridge, 78
Ortiz, Signe, 205
Oshoga, 17–19
Ottawa Lake, 9

Owen Park (Eau Claire, WI), 168, 175, 181

Pahquahwong (Ojibwe village), 7
paper mills, 42–43
Park Falls (WI), 42, 142
Park Theater (Hayward, WI), 75
Parkhurst, Helen, 194
Pat's Landing, 75
Paul Bunyan Logging Camp Museum,
    170–171, *170*
Pelican Lake, 33
Pepin, Lake, 8, 14, 191, 200
Pepin County Courthouse, *190, 193*, 194
Perkins, John E., 144
Peterhansel, Bernie, 51
Pfund, Henry, 35
Philleo, Florence "Floy," 43
Phoenix Park (Eau Claire, WI), 181, *182*
Pike, Rod, 161
Pike Lake, 80
Pile Driver (wrestling move), 36
pine tree log, largest, 25
Pioneer Girl (Wilder), 191
Poling, Jerry, 169
Polish immigrants, 26
Port Edwards Company, 44
Post, Village of (WI), 56, 75–76
Pottawatomie, 9
Pound, Ezra, 162–163
Pound, Thaddeus, 162, 167
Powell, Karen, 46, 47
Price, Jerry, 93, 179, 198
Price, Sterling (Confederate general), 145
Price Dam, 98, 100
Prince (horse), 73
printing equipment, 48
Pure Water Days (Chippewa Falls, WI), 164
Putnam, Henry C., 131

racetracks, 136–137
Radisson, Pierre-Esprit, 11–12, 56, 105
Radisson Flowage (lake), 92
railroads: frac sand trains, 110–111; and
    lumber industry, 28, 30, 106–107
Ramsey, Alexander, 17
Randy's Jim Town Inn, 141
rapids: and Carver's journey, 14, 177; East
    Fork trips, 33–34, 37, 55; and fishing,
    115; Little Falls dam tragedy (1905),

121–123, 124; role in fur trading, 157;
    of St. Mary River, 8; on trip to Jim Falls,
    134–136
Rasmussen, Charlie, 61
Rawls, Sophie, 128
Rawls, Wilson "Woody," 126–129, *129*
Reads Landing (MN), 187, 190, 200
Red Cedar River, 2, 26, 183, 189
Red Cliff Reservation, 19
Regez, Roger and Darlene, 168
Remembering Eau Claire (Arnold), 175
reservations, creation of, 19–20
reservoirs. *See* dams and dam building; *and
    individual reservoir names*
resorts, 55–56. *See also individual resorts*
Reyes, Denny, 59, 76, 82, 85
Rice Lake (WI), 98
Richardson, J. P., 172
Robert, Josephine, 130
Rock Fest (Cadott, WI), 141
Rogers, Robert, 13
Rosenburg, Bob, 141
Rosholt, Malcolm, 97, 124
Round Lake, 76, 80
rubber duck race fund-raiser, 88–89, 94,
    101, 102

Sacred Heart Church (Eau Claire, WI), 165
Sammy's Pizza, 169, 172
sand, and Chippewa River, 183–184,
    199–200
Sanders, Phyllis, 107
Sandy Lake (MN), 17
Sault Ste Marie, 8
Saulteur (French name for Ojibwe), 9
sawmills, 26, 27, 146, 153–154, *159*,
    166–167
Sawyer County Gazette, 61, 86
Sawyer County Historical Society, 68, 70, 72
Sawyer County Record, 68, 75, 86
Sawyer County (WI), 7, 56, 64, 85, 98,
    100, 106
Schoolcraft, Henry, 23–24
Schuster, Tony, 103, 150
Screaming Eagles (US Army unit), 145
Second Harvest (hunger relief charity), 102
self-reliance, emphasis on, 75, 102
Seymour Cray Sr. Blvd. (Chippewa Falls,
    WI), 161

Shake, Rattle, and Roll (Cadott, WI), 141
Shanagolden (WI), 42–45
Shanagolden Bridge, 32
Shanagolden Logging Company, 33
Shaw, Daniel, 184
Shoo-fly Landing (Ella, WI), 196, 198–199
Shydlowski, Blaire, *100*, 101–102
Silver Mine Hill ski jump, 185–186, *186*
skiers and skiing, 71–72, 185–186, *186*
Sky, Chief (Ahgamahwegezhig), 143
Soltis, Joe, 55
Spirit of the Ojibwe (Balbin), 62–64
Spray, Louie, 76
spring water, 162–163
St. Anthony Catholic church (Church
    Island), 79
St. Anthony Falls, 13
St. Croix Reservation, 19
St. Croix River, 2, 71
St. Germaine, Rick, 104–105, 196
St. Mary River, 8
St. Mary's of the Falls (church), 156
Stanchfield, Daniel, 15–16
Stanley brothers' sawmill, 146
steamboats, 186–187, 189–190
Steel Toed Shoes (business), 181
Stockfarm Bridge, 33
The Streams and Rivers of Minnesota
    (Waters), 4, 23–24
sturgeon (fish and fishing), 141, 160
Sturgeon Festival (Jim Falls, WI), 140–142
Summer Shandy (beer), 164
Sutherland, George, 14
Tainter, Edwin, 58–59
Taylor, Zachary, 16
Teal River, 78
Telemark Lodge, 71–72
Thames (river), 2
Thayer, Gordon, 65–68, *66*, 78, 80
Thayer, Thad, 56
Thornapple River, 98
Thorp, Karen, 47
Tietz, Matt and Susan, 179
Tiffany Wildlife Area, 197–198, 199
Timber Kove, 75
tire manufacturing, 179
trade and traders. *See* fur trade
treaties, Ojibwe and US government,
    15–20, 26, 41, 57, 78

Treeland Resorts, 72–75
Treeland's Cabins, 74
Treland, Cheryl, 72, 73–75, 82
Treland, Harold, 72–73, 74–75, 82
Treland, Oluf, 72, 73–74
Trout Fest (Exeland, WI), 94
Twain, Mark, 2–3, 189. *See also* Clemens, Samuel
Tyrone land restoration, 198

Union Lumber, 179
Uniroyal, 179, 181
US Army Corps of Engineers, 184, 200
US Army's 101st Airborne Division, 145
US Fish and Wildlife Service, 61
US Forest Service, 28, 40–42, 59, 68
University of Wisconsin–Eau Claire, 177–178, 205
University of Wisconsin–Stevens Point, 24, 194
"The Unknown Shore" (Hardy), 191
U.S. Rubber, 179

Valens, Richie, 172
Vanek, John, 13
Variety Vending, 180
Vernon, Justin, 173–174
veterans, recognition of, 46–48, *48*, 88, 111
Vilas, William F., 42–43
Villiard, Robert, 105
Visitor (tourist magazine), 70
Vivian (band), 174
Volume One (arts publication), 174

wall of honor (Winter, WI), 88
walleye fishing, 34, 75–76
Walters, Tim, 124
Wannigan Restaurant and Resort, 88–89, 94, 95
Warren, William, 9, 10, 197
Water Power Act (1920), 57, 203
Waters, Thomas F., 4, 23–24, 113
Watrous, John S., 17
Weigal, Jerry, 136
Weiss Community Library, 68
Wenabozhoo, 58
West Fork, Chippewa River, 6–7, 31, 77–78, 85
Western Union Telegraph Company, 131

Weyerhaeuser, Frederick, 98, 106, 120, 153–154, 179, 195
Where the Red Fern Grows (Rawls), 126, 128, 129
wild Chippewa, 118–137, *148*, 203
wild rice, 58, 149
Wilder, Laura Ingalls, 190–191
Williams, Jeff (astronaut), 86
Williams brothers (alias for Ed and Lon Maxwell), 192
wind problems, and canoeing, 53–54, 92, 119–120, 147–149
Windfall Lake, 103
Windigo Lake, 104
Wingerd, Mary Lethert, 15–16
Winter (WI), 7, 61, 85–88, 99–102
Winter Dam, 19–20, 56–60, 70, 94–97, *96*, 202
Winter Lake, 93
Winter Wonderland (variety store), 86
Winter Woods (Glidden, WI), 32
The Wisconsin (Derleth), 2
Wisconsin Central Railroad, 30, 31
Wisconsin DNR (Department of Natural Resources), 55, 59, 68, 76, 77, 113, 198, 204
Wisconsin Newspaper Association, 47
Wisconsin Rapids (WI), 42–44
Wisconsin-Minnesota Light and Power Company, 57, 59
Wise, Tony, 71–72
Wissota, Lake, 60, 123, 149–150, 154, 158
Wissota Dam, 57, 95
Wissota terrace (geological feature), 147
Wittwer, Andrea Marple, 68–70, 80–82
WJOB (radio station), 61
Wold, Elmer, 142
Wolf, William, 57–58
Wordsworth, William, 2
World Lumberjack Championship, 71–72
wrestling, professional, 34–36
Wurtzel, Norbert, 111, 178
Wyman, Walker, 27–28, 126, 143

Xcel Energy. *See also* Northern States Power (NSP): and Dells Dam, 168; effect of dams on river speed, 115; and relicensing of dams, 61, 113, 203–204; role in lake creation, 123; substation activities, 138–139; Tyrone land restoration, 198; and Winter Dam, 58–60, 94–97

Yellow River, 28, 158

Zach, Alvin, 47
Zeitlin, Richard, 143–144
Zinsli, Bonnie, 126
Zwiefelhofer, Jane, 128

About the Author

Richard D. Cornell started writing and journaling at a young age as a way to reflect on life and after retirement began publishing his work. He wrote the 2006 *Wisconsin Magazine of History* article "Knights of the Spike-soled Shoe: Lumbering on the Chippewa," and co-wrote with Jerry Poling the news feature "Greats of the Gridiron," about the undefeated 1906 Eau Claire High School football team. He also

PHOTO BY DIXIE CORNELL

self-published the memoir *Finding My Father*, about his quest to learn about his father, who was killed in World War II when Cornell was thirteen months old. Cornell's videos of his travels and interviews for this book can be found on his YouTube channel.